D1481897

DATE DUE

GREAT WRITERS JACK KEROUAC

GREAT WRITERS

CHARLES BUKOWSKI

JACK KEROUAC

BARBARA KINGSOLVER

SYLVIA PLATH

J.R.R. TOLKIEN

KURT VONNEGUT

JACK KEROUAC

Jenn McKee

Foreword by Toby Thompson

CHELSEA HOUSE
PUBLISHERS
A Haights Cross Communications ✦ Company
Philadelphia

CHELSEA HOUSE PUBLISHERS

VP, NEW PRODUCT DEVELOPMENT Sally Cheney
DIRECTOR OF PRODUCTION Kim Shinners
CREATIVE MANAGER Takeshi Takahashi
MANUFACTURING MANAGER Diann Grasse

Staff for JACK KEROUAC

EXECUTIVE EDITOR: Matt Uhler
ASSOCIATE EDITOR: Susan Naab
EDITORIAL ASSISTANT: Sharon Slaughter
PRODUCTION EDITOR: Megan Emery
SERIES AND COVER DESIGNER: Takeshi Takahashi
COVER: © Bettmann/CORBIS
LAYOUT: EJB Publishing Services

A Haights Cross Communications ✦ Company

http://www.chelseahouse.com

First Printing

9 8 7 6 5 4 3 2 1

Library of Congress Cataloging-in-Publication Data

McKee, Jenn.
  Jack Kerouac / Jenn McKee.
    p. cm.
  Includes bibliographical references and index.
  ISBN 0-7910-7845-0
  1. Kerouac, Jack, 1922-1969. 2. Authors, American—20th century—
Biography. 3. Beat generation—Biography. I. Title.

  PS3521.E735Z774 2004
  813'.54—dc22

                                    2004005876

▆▆▆▆▆ TABLE OF CONTENTS

IN 1959, DURING MY FIFTEENTH summer, I worked on a ranch near West Yellowstone, Montana, where I pulled barbed wire, cleared pasture, rode fenceline and endured the musings of a near-psychotic wrangler named Ray as he spun yarns and sang murder ballads in the bunkhouse. Meanwhile the ranch owner—daughter of a wealthy Long Island family—swilled martinis and shotgunned swallows from the eaves in Chinese pajamas, a silk turban and Arabian slippers with the toes pointed up. It was a confusing time. I was no Huck Finn lighting out for the territories, but a child of privilege with a roughneck job his parents had brokered. The two novels I'd packed were *Pride and Prejudice* and *The Dharma Bums*—the former, required reading at the prep school I attended, the latter all the bohemian rage. Jane Austen made me want to curl up and doze, but Jack Kerouac got my heart pounding and made me wild to be a writer.

Now, thirty-five years after his death, Jenn McKee's fine recounting of Kerouac's life reminds me of how deeply I yearned to emulate him. Not his hitchhiking, drug use, orgiastic sex or gleeful boozing, so much, as his fierce dedication to writing. As William Burroughs said, "Jack Kerouac was a writer. That is, he *wrote*." And Allen Ginsberg: "I don't know of any other writer who had more seminal influence than Kerouac in opening up the heart of the writer to tell the truth from his own secret personal mind." But in 1959, I had my ranch job. And this was Montana. As novelist Thomas McGuane wrote, "If you read Jack Kerouac and were of a certain age, you felt you owned the whole place ... He trained us in the epic idea that the region was America; and

that you didn't necessarily have to take it in Dipstick, Ohio, forever just because you were there when your hour had come
round ... It was called *On the Road.*" I was prepared to meet Wrangler Ray as Dean Moriarity, but when I lobbed Jack's Zennishness
at him he stared like I was a Communist.

Eventually my writing took the form of participatory nonfiction, or the New Journalism, a genre where the author is at
story-center practicing, as Ginsberg said of Jack's work, "[often] a
kind of prose which is neither fiction nor nonfiction, but is actually the mind of the writer thinking about the real world." That
practice led me to compose books about Dylan's hometown of
Hibbing, Minnesota, about FBI drug stings in Manhattan, about
glib survivors of the 1960's, and a reportorial memoir, *Saloon,*
about four years on the road, searching for the Great American
Bar. In West Yellowstone at fourteen, though, I identified less with
Jack's road-fueled exuberance than with his writerly sadness—that
exquisite melancholy that haunted him throughout his life.

As Ernest Hemingway said, the best early training for a writer
is "an unhappy childhood," and Jack trained hard. He was the son
of alcoholic parents, a non-English speaking French-Canadian in a
working class, New England town, a Catholic boy tormented by
his invalid brother's death, a guilt ridden omni-sexual and, as his
mother's darling, the object of incestuous ministrations (she
bathed him until he was twelve) and an enmeshment with her that
lasted until his death. McKee observes, rightly, that the pain of
these issues nudged Jack toward the cultivation of a rich fantasy
life, manifesting itself in various dissociative practices—one of
which was writing.

Much has been made of Kerouac's sociological impact—"when's
the last time you created a generation?" Seymour Krim asked, in
his preface to *Desolation Angels*—but I'd guess that *The Dharma
Bums* and *On the Road* were as important handbooks to my generation of writers as *The Sun Also Rises* and *Look Homeward Angel*
were to Jack's. They were tipsy with romance of the writerly life:
one of kicks, companionship, brooding solitude, word-drunk
prose, and a ceaseless examination of self. These are adolescent
preoccupations, to be sure. But also those of many adult novelists.

There's a closet writer in every reader ("I can do that"), but none keener than in the Kerouac devotee. Ginsberg was his acolyte, and it's fitting that through Allen's and Anne Waldman's efforts, a writing program—The Jack Kerouac School of Disembodied Poetics—was established at Naropa. For my adolescent self, Jack's influence came with *The Dharma Bums*. His alter-ego, Ray Smith, headed west (I already was in Montana) in search of inspiration and adventure, finding much of that in the company of Japhy Ryder, (Zen poet and environmentalist, Gary Snyder), on the slopes of California's Sierra mountains and in Washington's High Cascades. The novel featured wilderness backpackers, Frisco revelers, freight-train bhikkus, Tantric sex buffs, and scofflaw poetry ravers. But at its heart was an intense group of writers hanging out and *talking about writing*. (I would find my such group, later, in Livingston, Montana.) The book became a hearty bestseller—even Jackie Kennedy was photographed reading it on *Air Force One*—a fact hard to imagine in today's literary climate.

Kerouac was technically a novelist, but as McKee points out, at heart he was a memoirist, using "the creation of his novels as his own, public confessional," enlightening his readers "about his own desperate, strained inner life with painful candor." And I believe his greater influence may lie neither with his celebration of the beat vision, nor with his invention of "spontaneous bop prosody," but with his recasting of the literary memoir. Today, I teach in an MFA program; memoir writing is ninety percent of what nonfiction students wish to learn. But during the 1950's, it was the fictive way or the highway, as it was illegal to identify real people committing outrageous or even quietly personal acts in a work of literature. Those restrictions eased with Supreme Court rulings of the 1960's, and literary nonfiction exploded with the New Journalism, the New Biography and the New Memoir. The impact of Jack's candor, energy and stylistic zest upon writers as different as Tom Wolfe, Annie Dillard, Robert Stone, Hunter S. Thompson, Bob Dylan, Sam Shepard, and Mary Karr is obvious. As novelist William C. Woods has said, "Jack claimed his life would be a legend, and had the literary power to make that claim absolutely real."

But by the late sixties, he was too drunk and dispirited to care.

The damage to Kerouac's psyche from alcoholism—what Tom McGuane's called "the writer's black lung disease"—has been understressed. Jack drank himself to death at age forty-seven, but booze first affected him at home, as the child of alcoholic parents. Alcoholism is a family disease, injurious to a child's self-esteem, sense of autonomy, psychic integration, capacity to trust, and heightening his dissociative tendencies. Jack struggled with its effects to the finish. His drinking had more to do with those American (and alcoholic) anxieties McKee calls "the perpetual interior battle between cynicism and optimism, anarchy and control, freedom and security, hubris and self-doubt," than has been noted. Paradoxical behavior, such as Kerouac's belligerent anti-Semitism, while cherishing Jewish friends, adamant gay-bashing, while sporadically practicing homosexuality, and reactionary conservatism, while living apolitically, is classically alcoholic.

During the summer of 1956, Jack's sixty-three day stint without booze or drugs, as a fire lookout on Desolation Peak, proved the one extended period of sobriety in his adulthood. He wrote of it both in *Desolation Angels* and in *The Dharma Bums*. On Desolation Peak, he found something like serenity, "a vision of the freedom of eternity." The mountains, the rocky wilderness, "the void," as he called that landscape, became his higher power—a submission to which is indispensable for alcoholic recovery. Of that experience he'd write, in *Dharma*: "Desolation, Desolation, I owe so much to Desolation," and, "I have fallen in love with you, God. Take care of us all, one way or the other." If he'd nurtured that caring presence, rather than heading "down the trail back to this world," with its "humanity of bars and burlesque shows and gritty love, all upsidedown in the void," he might have survived.

On October 21, 1969, the news of his death reached me at home. I was typing the last pages of my Hibbing memoir, *Positively Main Street*, in which my character (a young writer in thrall to Bob Dylan) debated whether to mail off a magazine piece that would do much to dispel his hero's calculated mythos. This had been my first reportorial gambit on the road, and it had been wildly confusing. "Should I send it, should I send it?" I asked. I would, of course, but in the book's narrative, before leaving Hibbing and motoring east to Highway 61, I rummaged through my gear to find a Powr-House blue denim engineer's cap I'd bought on Howard Street. It was my good luck hat. At that moment, or close to it, a newscast interrupted my writing to report that Jack had died. I sat there motionless. Then I scrolled up the page and typed, "Jack Kerouac Is Dead?" as my final chapter head. The question might have fit anywhere.

Toby Thompson
April 2004

I CAME OF AGE SMACK DAB in the midst of Generation X—a demographic defined, per the late eighties media, by its world-weary cynicism, as well as for its dim chances of financially achieving as much or more than its immediate forbears. And true to form, I worked as a video store clerk and as a bookseller for minimum wage, feeling wholly underwhelmed by the corporate rat race opportunities available after earning my undergraduate degree in the early 1990s. I ate sparse meals (usually peanut butter sandwiches or microwaved Spaghettios) in a moldy, Ann Arbor basement apartment. I wore tie-dyed t-shirts with a cheap peace symbol necklace; struggled to make the rent and my car payment each month; heard the couple who lived above me fight daily; and cited Jack Kerouac as a kind of latter-day prophet, a modern Thoreau, who provided me and those like me with some small sense of empowerment.

Wait—have I mentioned that at the time, I hadn't read one word Kerouac had written?

Sad, but true, and not at all uncommon. With the sort of arrogance that only comes with the combination of youth and a recently-tendered liberal arts degree, I felt that I just knew in my gut, at my core, what Kerouac was all about, and this figure, what I thought he stood for, soothed me. He appeared to lend quiet nobility to my disillusionment and poverty, mirroring it back to me—as well as to all the other neo-hippies of the time—as a kind of valuable, to-thine-own-self-be-true existence. As Kerouac biographer Barry Miles noted, "the young people of the late eighties and nineties came of age in the long, dark ice age of Ronald

1

Reagan and Margaret Thatcher, an era of anti-drug hysteria and the rise of the religious right. This new generation, many of them born in the sixties, had to start all over again rediscovering archetypes and icons that they could use" (Miles, xii). Obviously, American youth at this time had become, once again, more than primed for a Beat renaissance, which resurrected Kerouac as a larger-than-life shaman, an atavistic symbol of self-love, experimentation, rebellion, and hard truths.

In reality, though, the very hardest truth is that between our assumed perception of Kerouac's "message" and his lived life there exists an impassable chasm of contradiction and infinite complexity, made all the more complicated by the fact that nearly all his works were autobiographies thinly disguised as fiction. Had I actually read Kerouac's works in college, however, I might well have noticed that in addition to his famous literary trademarks—defined by Miles as "worship of pure physical energy, of movement, exuberance, of the vitality, joy and spontaneity of youth, tinged with just a touch of sentimentality" (Miles, ix)—Kerouac's work also exhibited strong hints regarding the bleakness of the drifter/hipster lifestyle, thus quietly poking holes into its own professed, romantic illusion; I might have then detected how a thread of existential emptiness and grasping and madness worked to undermine, to some extent, the irresistible enthusiasm of the prose. Consider, for instance, this passage:

> I was far away from home, haunted and tired with travel, in a cheap hotel room I'd never seen, hearing the hiss of steam outside, and the creak of the old wood of the hotel, and footsteps upstairs, and all the sad sounds, and I looked at the cracked high ceiling and really didn't know who I was for about fifteen strange seconds. I wasn't scared; I was just somebody else, some stranger, and my whole life was a haunted life, the life of a ghost. (*On the Road*, 15)

Piercingly lucid and heartbreaking textual moments like this, in Kerouac's now-sacred Beat Generation bible *On the Road*, have never garnered as much attention from readers and critics as have the verbal jazz riffs, the seemingly celebratory hedonism, and the recounting of unabashed rebellions against America's suffocating, Puritanical social conventions. Obviously, though, behind the flash and innovation of the book's prose lay these clues regarding the Kerouac most people don't know—and probably wouldn't want to know, since it would destroy the romantic mythology that everyone, myself included, had subsequently created around him.

And naturally, the truth was far uglier than the myth, with Kerouac drinking himself to death in 1969 at the relatively young age of forty-seven. From early childhood, when his seemingly saint-like brother Gerard died of rheumatic fever, to his road adventures with Neal Cassady, Kerouac felt upstaged at every turn. Indeed, even when he finally did get his moment in the spotlight, receiving recognition as the media-appointed King of the Beats after the release of *On the Road,* he was profoundly overwhelmed by the public's assumptions and pre-constructed image of him—having already moved far away, intellectually and philosophically, from the perspective from which he originally wrote the book six years before—and soon, the traveling and wandering for which he is most celebrated became a stereotyped image he never escaped.

For like many who achieve fame in America, Kerouac was and has been reduced to a monolithic symbol, one embodying stock fantasies about a morally looser, anti-materialistic counterculture. In the foreword to David Sandison's Kerouac biography, Carolyn Cassady, a friend, occasional lover, and longtime fixture in Kerouac's life (as Neal Cassady's wife), pondered readers' and critics' misinterpretation—or manipulation—of Kerouac's ideas:

> In my efforts to understand Kerouac's increasing popularity, I have spoken to dozens of young people in the U.S. and Europe. They can seldom pin down their admiration in words, but one of the words often mentioned is "freedom." Ah, FREEDOM, what has that meant to successive generations? On the surface it appears to have developed since the Sixties into an acceptance of license then chaos, but there is no real freedom without fences. And that sort of "freedom" was not at all what Kerouac intended to transmit. (Sandison, 10)

Similarly, Kerouac's friend and biographer, Ann Charters, noted:

> To this generation Jack Kerouac became a romantic hero, an arche-
> typal rebel, the symbol of their own vanities, the symbol of their
> own romantic legend. He never understood this. He was a man
> whose life was directed by what he felt under his skin, not inside
> his head. If he had understood it he wouldn't have written it.
> (Charters, 22)

Clearly, Charters believes that Kerouac wrote in order to discover
the places, both dark and light, within himself rather than to propose a way of life for others. But as both of these passages indicate,
Kerouac's own identity fell from his control as soon as it entered
the public space, leaving the thin-skinned writer frustrated and
utterly bewildered. Such is the fate of our icons: they become, particularly in memory, what we want and need them to be. And in
truth, of course, Kerouac's "freedom," as referred to by Carolyn
Cassady, became a maddening labyrinth for him, leading him back
and forth across the country without an internal compass, and
without a single destination ever once providing him with a sem-
blance of long-term happiness.

And while Kerouac sought out sexual gratification from count-
less partners, and abused alcohol and drugs his whole life, he
nonetheless found the hippies of the sixties—who, by most
accounts, evolved as a direct consequence and spawn of Kerouac's
(and the other Beats') published works—to be lazy and repugnant.
As his friend William Burroughs, author of the novels *Junky* and
Naked Lunch, noted, "Kerouac had always been a political
paradox: a peace-loving Buddhist in an Eisenhower jacket, with a
prayer bell in one hand and a flamethrower in the other"
(Amburn, 327). Indeed, Kerouac's conservative Republican
beliefs, his racism, his anti-Semitism, his misogyny, his homophobia, his support for the Vietnam War, and even his distaste for
driving (he was never good at it) never fail to confound readers
who venture beyond his primary works.

As readers, of course, we tend to presume that authors have
motives, designs on how their artistic works should affect us,

perhaps going so far as to alter our perceptions, ideas, actions, or beliefs. But what happens when this presumption fails? Readers have always assumed that Kerouac must have intended to present a model for life when he wrote his books. But could Kerouac be holding his life up to the light for us to dissect but *not* emulate?

The latter possibility is particularly hard to swallow as a theory because of the seductive vibrancy of Kerouac's writing. In *On the Road*, for instance, he wrote: "What is that feeling when you're driving away from people and they recede on the plain till you see their specks dispersing?—it's the too-huge world vaulting us, and it's good-by. But we lean forward to the next crazy venture beneath the skies." Ultimately, Kerouac, despite including moments of loneliness in the text, made the whole enterprise of the happy wanderer sound just too exhilarating, too delicious for us to consider it as anything but a Siren song that means to draw us out into our beat up, old cars, chasing after Kerouac's taillights, joining him on the road to wherever.

In one of the last things Kerouac wrote before his death—a magazine article titled "After Me, the Deluge," which is now included in *The Portable Jack Kerouac*—he bristled at the notion of causing America's youth to follow in his footsteps:

> I'd better go around and tell everybody, or let others convince me, that I'm the great white father and intellectual forbear who spawned a deluge of alienated radicals, war protestors, dropouts, hippies and even "beats," and thereby I can make some money maybe and a "new Now-image" for myself (and God forbid I dare call myself the intellectual forbear of modern spontaneous prose), but I've got to figure out first how I could possibly spawn Jerry Rubin, Mitchell Goodman, Abbie Hoffman, Allen Ginsberg and other warm human beings from barrios and the blacks in their Big and Little Harlems, and all because I wrote a matter-of-fact account of a true adventure on the road (hardly an agitational propaganda account) featuring an ex-cowhand and an ex-footballer driving across the continent north, northwest, midwest and southland looking for lost fathers, odd jobs, good times, and girls and winding up on the railroad. Yup, I'd better convince myself that

these thinkers were not on an entirely different road. (*The Portable Jack Kerouac*, 573)

The sarcastic, bitter tone of this passage, in addition to information gleaned from biographies and interviews, clearly demonstrates that our inherent assumptions about Kerouac's intentions and values are decidedly wrong. Carolyn Cassady wrote: "Jack lived in a fantasy world ... He expressed his opinions spontaneously and they often conflicted with each other. He never followed a single thread, and it's this habit of inconsistency that makes it so hard for people to determine what he actually thought" (Sandison, 67). Obviously, Kerouac's resentment regarding the credit and the blame he received from both ends of the political spectrum—in his view, mistakenly—helped fuel his intense misery in his last years. As always, Kerouac felt as though no one ever really "got" him.

Since that time, however, many have tried. Contradictions between who readers and critics thought Kerouac was, based on the content of his writing, and who he seemed to be in person may be at least partly explained by acknowledging Kerouac's constant feelings of shame and self-loathing. Heavily influenced by his Catholic upbringing, Kerouac used the creation of his novels as his own public confessional, reporting his actions while crippled, in his personal life, by the emotional and intellectual self-flagellation that accompanied them all. But despite, or perhaps because of, Kerouac's inconsistencies regarding his memoir-novels and his life, a particularly large number of biographies have been published, each attempting to solve the riddle of Jack.

The task seems Herculean when readers learn that even Kerouac's closest friends appear to have been baffled by the man. One biographer noted that once, near the end of Kerouac's life, Beat poet Gregory Corso came out to Jack's home, and the two men got into an argument about civil rights. Corso argued that moments in *On the Road* would appear to belie Kerouac's racism, but Kerouac maintained that "'poetic statements' in artistic works did not commit him to them in his personal life" (Amburn, 326). In the same vein, biographer Ann Charters responded to such discrepancies and contradictions with this explanation: "as [Kerouac] wrote it down the legend became, finally, the only reality his life had" (Charters, 22). Thus, despite Kerouac's method of spontaneous prose and his constant striving for unadulterated truth, there were always details and facts that fell between the lines of his own subjective filter; the impulse that produced a thought at any given time was never guaranteed to stabilize, but rather changed instantly, more often than not. Clearly, there were acts and spoken words and a sense of culpability that Kerouac couldn't face up to himself, let alone admit to a seemingly enigmatic, judgmental world.

Kerouac once stated during an interview: "I wasn't trying to create any kind of new consciousness ... We were just a bunch of guys who were out trying to get laid." (Amburn, 361). Though too glib to be wholly believed or taken seriously, this statement indicates Kerouac's uneasiness with his role as a cultural progenitor of the "tune in, turn on, drop out" generation. In another instance, Kerouac planned to speak to prisoners while Neal Cassady was serving time for drug possession, but he not only filched out on this obligation, he refused to ever visit the man who had been his closest friend, hero, and inspiration while he served his sentence. The reason? Kerouac was scared that the press would interpret his visit to San Quentin as an endorsement of drugs and lawbreaking. Both of these responses, of course, seem ridiculous as one learns more and more about Kerouac's spoken words, actions, behavior, and addictions, particularly across the span of his lifetime.

He abused drugs and alcohol to the end, he confesses, in his books, to stealing on occasion, and he and Neal hurt people emotionally everywhere they went; it was part of their modus operandi, and one of the many not-so-ideal consequences of living purely by impulse. Kerouac's lack of objectivity and self-awareness aside, however, the point that we must take from these examples is clear: Kerouac's work, in retrospect, simply seems to attempt to capture the romantic idealism, energy, and restlessness of youth rather than suggest we live our whole life in this frenetic manner. We all grow up, as Kerouac did, and innocence is always lost when we learn that our daydreams are unworkable or, at the very least, far overrated. Kerouac simply managed, through his work, to bottle and preserve that hopeful moment, which makes it both a blessing and a curse. Because in books we can experience this moment as many times as we want to read it, Kerouac's prose gave it the impression of permanence, though the man who wrote it continued, by necessity, to evolve and lose more illusions about himself and the world, just as everyone does.

Thus we must realize that Kerouac, rather than freezing himself inside a particular moment that he advocated for all, simply wanted to be a writer and tell America, and the world, about his own desperate, strained inner life with painful candor. And though he died with only one true, bona fide literary "hit"—that being, of course, *On the Road*—he was extremely prolific in his lifetime and left an indelible mark on writing, and American society at large, that would have surpassed even his most grandiose fantasies.

Truly, in many ways, a man before his time, Kerouac now appears to have been the important kick-off point for many of today's fads, obsessions, and interests in America. To name a few examples: he explored, researched, and wrote books on the subject of Buddhism, presaging the New Age movement—perhaps even inspiring it, in part—by many years, fighting to introduce the West to the ideas of the East at a time when few people were interested; raised the issue of God and spirituality consistently, making it clear that he did not view his "Beat" ideas and behavior as a threat to his staunch religious faith; wrote about a mixed-race relationship in *The Subterraneans*, breaking a powerful societal taboo; emphasized the importance of nature in *The Dharma Bums*, presciently raising the topic of environmentalism and conservation; inspired fashion trends, along with Neal Cassady, that still linger—most notably, the popularity of blue jeans, t-shirts, and flannel shirts, emphasizing comfort over formality in day-to-day clothing; helped literature and poetry evolve into a performance art, often re-aligning it with music and performing in easily accessible coffee houses and nightclubs (thus de-institutionalizing and defrocking poetry's previously stuffy, ivory tower image); re-vitalized travel writing as a genre, which came to spawn the New Journalism; created a composition method called "spontaneous prose," which championed uncorrected, stream of consciousness writing as a means of extracting the hardest, purest, most honest thought from a writer's mind; and has now, for generations, provided individuals—including, in their time, Jacqueline Kennedy Onassis, Janis Joplin, Ken Kesey, Amiri Baraka, and Hunter S. Thompson—with an energetic, youthful, vernacular voice that seemed to speak directly to them in a way nothing else had, eliminating the distance that had always previously existed between writer and reader, changing their lives forever. Reportedly, even the pop music world was forever affected; one Kerouac biographer explained that John Lennon, during a phone conversation with the King of the Beats, stated that the spelling of "Beatles" stemmed in part from the band members' interest in this artistic youth movement in America.

As is always true, of course, a book is what readers make of it, and they continue to make Kerouac's work a touchstone of American youth culture, projecting onto it, and taking from it, what they want. And while this may certainly be part of the excitement of writing and reading and publishing, Kerouac flinched at the ever-widening gap between his public image and reality. He told biographer and editor Ellis Amburn that in the first blush of *On the Road* success—when fans assumed Kerouac to be the wild, raw Dean Moriarty character rather than the more withdrawn Sal Paradise narrator, for whom he was actually the model—he consistently disappointed readers. "The way they talked to me made me feel like an imposter," he told Amburn (277), a statement that resonates far beyond its original context. For the reason Kerouac was unhappy when he wasn't traveling was that it was at such times that he was forced to confront, and just be with, himself—a man he never learned to like much or even tolerate. Such self-loathing would seem to explain why he once wrote, and consistently believed again and again, that in order for him to survive, to keep living and breathing and pressing on, "The only thing to do was go."

CHAPTER ONE

Ti Jean

For the first four years of my life, while he lived, I was not Ti Jean Duluoz, I was Gerard, the world was his face, the flower of his face, the pale stooped disposition, the heartbreakingness and the holiness and his teachings of tenderness to me, and my mother constantly reminding me to pay attention to his goodness and advice.

—Jack Kerouac, *Visions of Gerard*

ONE OF THE WRITERS WHO initially sparked Jack Kerouac's passion to write, while he was a young man, was Thomas Wolfe; two of that author's works—*Look Homeward, Angel* and *You Can't Go Home Again*—have titles that, in a way, significantly sum up one important aspect of Kerouac's protracted suffering: a sense of frustrated nostalgia regarding his home and childhood.

Throughout his life, Kerouac ruminated on, and romanticized, his boyhood and adolescence in Lowell, a poor mill-town in Northeast Massachusetts, and this tendency toward nostalgia drove him to write books that would ultimately fit together as a single, epic work that bore witness to the course, and travails, of one man's life (thus emulating another of Kerouac's literary heroes: Marcel Proust). Kerouac harvested a great deal of writing material from his experiences in Lowell (resulting in *Visions of Gerard, Dr. Sax, Maggie Cassidy, The Town and the City,* and *Vanity of Duluoz* among others), and although he bounced back and forth across the country in nomadic fashion most of his life, his hometown was the on-again, off-again, love/hate security-blanket destination to which he often returned. (Of course, like every other destination, it never satisfied him for long; reality always, inevitably, failed to live up to his memories and imaginings.)

In the introduction to his book *Lonesome Traveler,* Kerouac cited Breton, France as the land of his forefathers. He also claimed that in 1750, his Kerouac ancestor, a baron of Cornwall, Brittany, was the recipient of a land grant in Canada. While this link to royalty has since been largely de-bunked, Kerouac clearly believed the story that had been handed down to him, and he held fast to this image of his regal, stalwart forebears as a source of family pride and identity. As is often the case, however, the truth mixed with myth to the point of confusion regarding Kerouac's true heritage. While it seems quite likely that Canadian Indians married into the Kerouac family after they migrated to Quebec—thus providing Jack with some fraction of Native American blood—it seems sketchy, at best, that the family had consisted of "aristocratic descendants of Cornish Celts who had come to Cornwall from Ireland" in ancient times, as Jack's father had told him (Charters, 24).

Gabrielle L'Evesque and Leo Kerouac—Jack's Quebec-born parents—met and married each other only twelve miles outside of Lowell in 1915. Leo's father, Jean-Baptiste, had been the son of potato farmers in Quebec, and shortly after Leo was born in 1889, Jean-Baptiste moved his family to Nashua, New Hampshire. There, Jean-Baptiste, a carpenter, prospered with a lumbering business, and as a result, Leo received an excellent private school education in Rhode Island, while his six younger siblings, four of whom were reportedly either physically or mentally incapacitated, attended parochial school. With this solid academic training, Leo first found work in Nashua as a reporter and typesetter for a local French language newspaper, *L'Impartial;* later, however, his boss sent him to Lowell, where he lived with relatives and assumed nearly all responsibility for a similar, but financially failing, French language publication called *L'Etoile.*

And although he was settled in Lowell, Leo briefly returned to Nashua in 1915 to court and marry Gabrielle L'Evesque, a pretty, plump, dark-eyed, black-haired Catholic orphan whose life thus far had been far from easy. Her family had immigrated to New Hampshire from Quebec when Gabrielle was a small child, and not only did her mother die young, but her mill-worker-turned-tavern-keeper father died as well, in 1909, when Gabrielle was only fourteen years old. Left thus alone in the world at a young age, Gabrielle worked as a housemaid for aunts and uncles, then began working on a skiving machine in a shoe shop, cutting out pieces of leather and permanently blackening her fingertips. Gabrielle did this sort of work on and off throughout her entire life; ironically, though, biographers generally report that Gabrielle primarily married Leo in hopes of escaping a life of servitude.

Regarding Gabrielle's heritage, one of Gabrielle's grandmothers was half-Iroquois, and this was something that Jack fully embraced as a means of aligning himself, in blood and in spirit, with what he called the "Fellaheen" of the world. Biographer Tom Clark, regarding the primitive peoples to whom Jack thought himself strongly linked, noted that they "were, as [Kerouac] felt himself to be, instinctive beings, guided by mother wit, tuned in with the cosmic beat, and totally devoid of the modern sense of nationhood" (Clark, 5). Jack's fixation on dark-skinned native peoples and their cultures carried through much of his work (*Tristessa, Mexico City Blues, The Subterraneans,* "The Mexican Girl," etc.), in spite of the racism he seemed to have inherited from his parents.

Seven years before Jack's birth, Gabrielle and Leo settled in Lowell soon after their wedding, where Leo sold insurance for a short time. Eventually, he opened his own print shop called Spotlight Print, where he wrote and designed handbills and printed tickets for movies and vaudeville shows (years later, his children would see local shows for free, as a result, including stage shows with the Marx Brothers and W.C. Fields, before they began to appear in films); he also produced his own small-circulation newspaper (*The Lowell Spotlight*), which carried critical reviews of local theatrical productions, and sometimes worked at the town's social club, which was a bowling alley. Leo, always fearlessly outspoken, also began regularly contributing columns about local politics to another publication called *Focus,* wherein he regularly railed against the local government and its leaders with abandon. Kerouac biographer Barry Miles described Leo, Jack's model for masculinity, in the following manner:

> He was a well-known figure in the town though not necessarily well-liked: muscular, short, stocky, overweight, loud, verbose, opinionated, bigoted, leaving a trail of cigar smoke behind him as he stamped from place to place. He was a sporting man who followed the horses and managed a few semi-pro wrestlers and boxers, promoting the occasional fight. He was a classic small-town personality. A big fish in a small pond. (Miles, 7)

Despite Leo's various business interests and pursuits, however, getting by in Lowell was hard, and on March 12, 1922, Leo's last child, Jean-Louis Lebris de Kerouac, entered the world of the economically depressed textile town at a time when the rest of the country basked in the vibrant, decadent hedonism of the Roaring Twenties.

Jack spent his first two years with his family in a clapboard house on Lupine Road, and though most houses in the area were quite similar, the Kerouacs moved often, striving constantly for the American Dream of a better life, and the chance to get ahead, while also contending with intermittent financial woes. Jack was the youngest of three children; his brother Gerard, whose idealized memory would haunt Jack his whole life, was five when Jack arrived, while Caroline (called "Nin" by the family) was three. The siblings, and the parents, soon came to call Jack, the new baby, Ti Jean (Little Jean), a pet name that would stick with him permanently.

Jack always liked to tell others that his surname (which Leo translated as "Language of the House") carried with it the motto, "Aimer, Travailler, et Souffrir" (Love, Work, and Suffer); supposedly, this slogan had been embossed on the blue and white family shield, which Leo claimed the family acquired after migrating to Brittany from Cornwall. The veracity of this claim notwithstanding, the family members took the motto, particularly the last word ('suffer'), to heart, obsessed with the idea that pre-determined, terrible fates circumscribed their lives; it's thus no surprise to learn that Leo, Gabrielle, and, eventually, Jack's alcoholism always seemed, to them, never to be the root of any of their problems or unhappiness. In their minds, they drank because a life of misery was encoded in their DNA, wholly missing "the chicken or the egg" problem posed by the situation.

The town's economy, of course, did little to dissuade them against the notion that suffering was indeed the core of their collective, pre-ordained fate. Significantly, the localized depression, in which forty percent of Lowell's residents were on some form of welfare at once, had actually worked, in a way, toward perpetuating Jack's childhood ignorance regarding the English language. Years before his birth, immigrants from a number of countries who were willing to work for low wages had poured into the town of Lowell when times grew particularly tough; as a result, specific parts of the town had evolved into self-contained centers of foreign culture, linked by a common Catholicism but otherwise isolated by way of having their own stores/businesses, churches, schools, customs, and language. These separate areas made for anything but a melting pot atmosphere, however, and ethnic divisions and prejudices were common.

In addition to sections composed of Poles, Greeks, and Irish, there was an area called Centralville, or "Little Canada," that was populated by residents who hailed from French-speaking Quebec, most of whom spoke in a bastardized New England dialect called "joual." As a result of these self-imposed efforts to siphon off like with like, in terms of ethnicity, Jack's family and friends all communicated in joual, such that Jack spoke nothing else until he began his formal schooling at the age of five. (Many have noted, too, that even at fourteen, Kerouac still spoke English haltingly with a heavy accent, and that he didn't seem wholly comfortable with the language until adulthood; critics and biographers have speculated that this made Kerouac all the more sensitive to the

English language's cadences, rhythms, and meaning, since he had always had to work harder than most to decipher the language for himself.)

A year before his introduction to English, however, Jack suffered an experience at the age of four that he would write about, and think about, all the years of his life. Though spoiled and doted on by his family, dark-eyed Jack was, from his birth, overshadowed by the wraith-like, sickly, often bed-ridden presence of his older brother Gerard. Born with a rheumatic heart, well before the advent of heart valve transplants and penicillin, the boy was renowned for his gentleness, compassion, and piety; even though Gabrielle went to church daily to light a candle and educated all of her children in the ways of Catholicism—placing pictures of the young, consumptive nun St. Therese, who died of tuberculosis, around the house and teaching them all how to pray to her— Gerard was extraordinarily devout for a child and reportedly demonstrated a seriousness and grace that Gabrielle, as well as the local nuns, found moving. More typical of a big brother, though, Gerard also told Jack terrifying ghost stories to frighten him, and Kerouac later wondered, in a letter to Neal Cassady, whether Gerard actually despised Jack for his good health and fortune. But there were also times when Gerard felt better.

When well enough, the tall, pale, sandy-haired boy often took Jack, contrastingly strong and dark-featured, to a local grotto, where each of the twelve stations of the cross were displayed in glass cases; he also tried to teach his younger brother to love and respect animals, once releasing a mouse from a trap in front of him. Some of these accounts of Gerard's brief life, however, are over-inflated and hyperbolic to the point of resembling a fairy-tale, wherein, supposedly, birds befriended Gerard and sat on his windowsill during the particularly dark times of his illness; though such stories appear obviously overwrought, it's clear from Kerouac's written reflections that he accepted them as literal truths.

Kerouac, in his book *Visions of Gerard*, recounts the experience of knowing and losing his sanctified older brother. Readers should realize, though, that since Kerouac was four years old at the time Gerard died, much of this account was likely spoon-fed to him by others, primarily Gabrielle; by all accounts, she constructed Gerard as an impossibly tough act to follow, to the point that Jack's very existence and identity appear to have disappeared or, at the very least, mixed with that of his brother.

Just as Kerouac's legacy and life have been manipulated to fulfill readers' fantasies and needs since his death, so, clearly, had been Gerard's. But despite the Christ-like stories and anecdotes that fill Kerouac's extensive encomium—including one in which Gerard brings home a dirty, impoverished boy in order to feed him— Gerard's presence often seems quietly threatening and creepy, made more so when readers learn that Gerard, a few days before his death, slapped Jack hard across the face. In typical Jack-fashion, however, he turned this into an event that demonstrated his own culpability, fearing in that moment, he subconsciously wished for, and therefore caused, Gerard's early death; as he explained in a letter to Nin, "ever since, mortified beyond repair, warped in my personality and will, I have been subconsciously punishing myself and failing at everything" (Sandison, 21).

According to *Visions of Gerard*, the young boy's death occurred shortly after the family had moved again, this time to Beaulieu Street, after only one year on Burnaby Street. At school one day, Gerard fell asleep at his desk, telling nuns afterward that he had dreamed of white lambs pulling a wagon with the Virgin Mary, her billowing white robes held up by the beaks of bluebirds; apparently, she had come to take Gerard to heaven. He went home that day to face what would be his last long bout with his illness, and at his deathbed, over the course of two months, nuns clamored around the boy to note his dying words, despite the horrific nature of Gerard's mortal end; as was common for rheumatics, he bled uncontrollably, such that his skin turned purple and he suffocated, eventually choking on his own blood.

But the stories from Gerard's life confronted Jack again and again, and the message seemed clear: Gerard had been special and was the one who should have lived; as a point of comparison, Jack could never, and would never, match up, and thus began a pattern in Jack's life, wherein he felt destined/doomed to play second fiddle to someone more talented, charming, smarter, more vibrant, or just generally "better" than he could ever imagine himself being. Even in *Visions of Gerard*, Jack noted his feelings of jealousy over small things, like Gerard getting his breakfast first every morning, and stated outright, "There's no doubt in my heart that my mother loves Gerard more than she loves me." But despite this sort of petty, commonplace sibling envy, Gerard's death fueled Jack's larger, lifelong quest for spirituality, as well as his search for male guidance and companionship, thus laying the groundwork for two obsessions of Kerouac's life and work.

Following Gerard's death, Gabrielle suffered a nervous breakdown at the age of twenty-nine, causing many of her teeth to fall out; and although she eventually returned to work as a skiver—she had quit her job when she began having children—her marriage, which hadn't been an ideal match from the start, deteriorated rapidly. For his part, Jack, though only a child, also suffered grief with powerful intensity. According to Kerouac biographer Ellis Amburn, Jack "somehow convinced himself that a movie was being made of his life and that cameramen were following him everywhere. He even made up a title for the film, *The Complete Life of a Parochial School Boy*" (Amburn, 13). Jack also, at this time, reportedly saw spots; imagined he saw religious statues' eyes move, watching him; grew scared of shadows and the dark; and refused to sleep alone, staying glued to his mother night after night. According to Miles,

> For the first few ... months ... Jack would sit motionless in the parlour, in a daze, doing nothing. He grew increasingly pale and thin. But then, as the horrendous events passed into memory, he began to play again, though now he played alone and with more introspection—his older sister Nin had her own girlfriends. He played the old family Victrola and acted out movie scenarios to the music, some of which he developed into long serial sagas, to be 'continued next week'. In one of them the plot led to the hero being left tied up with rope, so Jack tied himself up and rolled around on the grass where the local children, coming home from school, saw him and laughed and thought he was crazy. (Miles, 13)

Clearly, Jack's melancholy and grief lingered, despite Gabrielle's best efforts, which included trips with him to Coney Island and the Roxy in New York, and hanging the "Jack be nimble" rhyme up on the wall in Jack's room. None of it inspired him back to normality or action right away, and during the course of these years, he created solitary games, including horse races that he performed in his room with marbles and a ruler, as well as a highly complex baseball game he created and played with a deck of cards. He kept careful records and statistics of the imagined horses and players, going so far as to create a racing sheet (with which he was familiar, thanks to Leo) that reported on the horses' performances; in this way, solitary Jack's first deep forays into the world of his imagination began at a young age.

One person who succeeded in fascinating Jack, though, came in the unlikely form of Leo's Sunday chauffeur. Armand Gauthier, a soft-spoken, thoughtful man so strong that he accidentally tore the arm from one of Leo's printing presses, became a professional wrestler, and Leo, who opened a boxing gym in 1930, assumed responsibility as his manager. When Gauthier came for dinner, Jack and Nin both delighted in playing with him, swinging from his flexed biceps. Gauthier was thus the first man, in Jack's world, to rise to hero status from outside the family, and inspired by him, Jack soon pursued arm wrestling matches with other boys—contests that may have acted as a first step toward Jack's development as a competitive athlete.

But before Jack grew more concentrated on the speed and strength of his body, he skipped the sixth grade, thanks to his strong academic performance, and was introduced to a new school: Bartlett Junior High, wherein teachers taught lessons only in English, all day each day (his previous school conducted classes half the day in joual, half in English), and students from all the different ethnic areas of Lowell attended. It was Jack's first real foray outside the insular French world of Pawtucketville and although Gabrielle disapproved, he began making friends with boys of different backgrounds, aligning himself particularly with the Greeks, whose work ethic and emphasis on learning was deemed similar to that of the children of Jewish immigrants.

Despite these new peers, however, Jack was by and large a loner, and one night in 1934, he had his fear of the dark re-instated when he saw, while walking with Gabrielle, a man carrying a watermelon on the Moody Street Bridge who suddenly collapsed and died in front of him, sending Jack back to the comfort of Gabrielle's bed in order to sleep at night.

An activity that comforted and entertained Jack at this time, though, was reading. Jack spent hours each week pouring over new Street & Smith published pulp serials that he bought at the local candy store; specifically, Jack faithfully devoured new titles in a series about a character named the Shadow. A precursor to many of the classic comic book heroes—and the basis for successful radio plays and theater serials, in addition to books and magazines—the Shadow wore a black slouch hat and a black cloak, sported two .45s, could make himself invisible, and fought evildoers in the night (laughing madly when he triumphed over them once again); according to the mythology, the Shadow could sniff out and detect these villains because he intrinsically knew better than others, "what evil lurks in the minds of men."

One reason for Jack's fascination with the series may well have been that it played to his very worst fears—born at the time of Gerard's death—about darkness; in this way, the character of the Shadow provided the world of Jack's own personal terror with a force of good that would protect rather than harm. The series also inspired Jack to compose his own comic books, stories, and—at age eleven, after reading Mark Twain's *Huckleberry Finn*—a novel called *Mike Explores the Merrimack*. Next, Jack penned a Jack London-inspired novel about an engineer in the Rocky Mountains, which he scribbled down, as he did all his projects, in nickel notebooks—a writing practice that he would continue to use throughout his life.

In the spirit of the Shadow, Jack also began to play out his comic book fantasies at night, outdoors. Originally, he played this game with a pair of brothers, Mike and Pete Houde, who encouraged him to join them in scaling trees, frightening pedestrians, and "breathing fire" (by way of spitting kerosene from their mouths). After some time, however, Jack struck out on his own as

"The Black Thief," wearing his father's battered fedora and Nin's black and red rubber beach cape; sometimes, he would commit small thefts—toys, articles of clothing—from nearby households and leave notes wadded up in cans. According to childhood friend, G.J. Apostolos, "one time [Jack] was the Silver Tin Can. If there was a window open, or a door, he'd throw a tin can through it with a note: 'The Silver Tin Can Strikes Again!'" (Gifford and Lee, 10). Not surprisingly, it was at this time that Jack made up imaginary characters, one of them being Dr. Sax, the figure who later inspired him, at age thirty-five, to write a book of the same name. In that novel, Sax is a clownish detective character with a green complexion; he fights (sometimes humorous) forces of evil, and the character "Jacky" is the only one who can see and communicate with Sax. (Critics have noted that while Dr. Sax's evident model, the Shadow, plowed down his enemies with guns, Dr. Sax is much more introspective, appearing as a student of the evil around him rather than a simple eradicator.)

Given Jack's volatile home life, it's no wonder the young boy created a cast of imaginary characters with whom he could escape from his circumstances. For in addition to moving often from house to house in different parts of town, and Gabrielle and Leo's alcoholism and constant bickering about Leo's gambling, whoring, and money-squandering, Gabrielle also refused to acknowledge, and thus adapt to the fact, that Jack was growing out of childhood. Most notably, Gabrielle insisted on bathing Jack until, when he was twelve years old, she caused him to have an erection while in the tub. This both infuriated Gabrielle, who chastised Jack and preached to him about the evils of the body, and embarrassed Jack, who, of course, had no physical control of such things as an adolescent. This horrible moment haunted Kerouac in dreams for the rest of his life and forever reinforced, as did Catholicism, the indelible link between shame and sexuality in Jack's mind.

Soon, though, another means of escape from Jack's home life arose: sports. A neighborhood baseball team formed among his friends, as did a football team, and Jack even jerry-rigged an old Victrola for the purposes of making a timer to record his friends', and his, track performances. Jack, though neither tall nor stocky, was strong and fast, with powerful legs, and as he began to play football informally with his friends, he recognized early on that he had more talent for the game than others. Soon, the boys wanted to pursue the game more seriously, so in 1935, Jack and one of his friends sent a letter of challenge to the *Lowell Sun*, asking local football teams to play them. They got responses, and in the first organized game, Jack, the youngest player on the field, ran at will, scoring no less than nine touchdowns.

Just after Jack started down the path to becoming a local star athlete, however, a natural disaster struck the town of Lowell. In 1936, when Jack was fourteen, a flood ravaged parts of the town, with water reaching levels as high as thirteen feet in some areas. Leo's print shop was hit, and although the damage wasn't monumental, it nonetheless caused Leo to lose his business; he was uninsured and his finances were, by way of his myriad vices, precarious enough to be felled by nearly anything. Once again turning to alcohol as a means of escape, Leo drank to the point of having to be carried home. Ever the conspiracy theorist, Leo stubbornly maintained that his business had been taken from him for political reasons, stemming from his fiercely critical columns in *Focus*, thus shifting the blame from himself, as he always did. Jack, being more spiritual, viewed the flood in a biblical context, seeing it as disaster visited upon sinners—specifically, himself; in this way, his future and that of the town mingled together, in his mind, making such acts of nature an externalization of his interior life.

But regardless of the causes, with the family's circumstances thus compromised, the Kerouacs moved once again, this time to the top floor of a tenement house on Moody Street, above a diner. There, in a poorer part of town, Leo carried water buckets for the WPA, then tried to get printing jobs, a pursuit which often led him to make trips out of town. Jack, meanwhile, continued to make new friends of various ethnicities and backgrounds, most of whom, predictably, Gabrielle disapproved of as being "beneath" her son.

One of Jack's friends who Gabrielle likely disapproved of was a Greek boy named Sebastian "Sammy" Sampas, a boy who not only shared Jack's interest in reading and writing—sometimes, reportedly, wearing a laurel wreath in his hair on the street as a teenager—but who was a member of a literary group Jack joined called the "Scribblers' Club," an organization run by a teacher at Bartlett Junior High School who recognized Jack's intellectual potential. Though many of the other boys viewed Sammy as a "sissy," and though he was often, as the sensitive, emotional type, the recipient of pranks and taunting, Jack reportedly came to his rescue once, staring down a group of bullies in his defense; for this, Sammy was eternally grateful and doggedly loyal.

In the same year as the flood in Lowell, another significant event occurred when Jack was fourteen years old. He visited a local priest named Armand "Spike" Morissette—a man who once hoped that Jack might consider a career in the priesthood, since the young man seemed serious and thoughtful about his religion. On this day, though, Morissette's first sight of Jack indicated that the boy was unnerved and in a fragile state. When the priest asked Jack what was wrong, Jack told him that his friends picked on him because he wanted to be a writer. Not surprisingly, these other boys thought the pursuit to be "sissy," just as they had assessed Jack's friend Sammy to be. This prejudice against writing as an occupation was not only maintained by Jack's friends, but re-inforced by nearly everyone around him.

In Lowell, a working class town wherein most of the French Canadian children spent their childhoods mentally preparing themselves for a life in the mill, Jack seemed an oddball, espe-cially to his own parents; due to Gabrielle's impoverished upbringing, she, in particular, wanted to climb her way into the upper middle class by way of the hard, practical work of her only remaining son, while Leo, too, scowled and grumbled about Jack's desired vocation, remarking often that Jack would have to be supported all his life. (Unfortunately, Leo hit fairly close to the mark regarding this last prognostication.) But Father Morrisette told Jack that personally, he didn't find the boy's dream to write amusing; in fact, he found himself deeply touched by the boy's nobility and earnestness. Morissette suggested that Jack go to New York, where one could make connections and get an education, and when Jack claimed poverty, the priest recommended earning a scholarship. Jack became focused on this, switching to the college prep track at his school (the only one to do so among his friends), and trying out that year for the football team at Lowell High.

A gifted student despite his initial language difficulties, Jack was younger and smaller than many of the other boys—due to having skipped a grade—making the enterprise of making the team exceedingly difficult at first. In fact, on the first day of practice, Jack, a sophomore, reportedly collapsed and threw up in front of the other players, missed his bus home, and stumbled there only to doze at the dinner table, his face in his plate—an inauspicious start, to say the least. And though Jack was stubborn and worked hard, he would not play that year, nor the next. Leo, as usual, smelled a conspiracy, but Jack, to his credit, kept his nose to the grindstone, determined to get better and earn respect.

Meanwhile, in school, despite his scholarship goal, Jack grew bored and restless with classroom learning and started skipping classes in favor of going to the library. There, he read literature voraciously, and his power of retention regarding details and facts was so impressive that his friends gave him the nickname "Memory Babe," a moniker in which Jack took great pride all his life. Naturally, Jack stuck out from his football friends because of his high-minded academic pursuits, but as a result of this propensity, he gained a reputation as a mama's boy, so fixated had he become on education as providing a means of pleasing her.

But the one peer who not only encouraged but shared in Jack's academic zeal was Sammy, who by then wished to be an actor. In the Young Prometheans, a discussion group that tackled issues of politics, philosophy, and literature (an outgrowth of the Scribblers' Club) and to which both boys belonged, they read political tracts about communism and Hitler and talked about social change and its obstacles, stretching their minds further than most Lowell residents ever would. To Jack, Sammy appeared to represent what was vibrant and hopeful and exciting—that is, all that the mill-town was not—and thus promised new thrills and ideas beyond the boundaries Jack had not yet been able to cross.

During Jack's senior season in football, he finally got to leave the sidelines and make game-winning plays, though he still did not start. He ran well with the ball, but he played poor defense and had

a tendency to drop balls; this, combined with the fact that substitu-
tions, at that time, happened rarely in football games, led to him
being the twelfth man on the team, a flashy position sometimes
referred to as "climax runner." The team won their first five games
that season without even getting scored on by their opponents, but
then they floundered until reaching their last game with their old
rival, Laurence. In that gridiron showdown, in November, 1938,
Jack scored a last minute touchdown, making him a local hero and
earning him scholarship offers from Frank Leahy, Boston College's
coach, who would soon be leaving for Notre Dame, and Lou Little,
Columbia's coach. (Both offers, however, came with complicated
business strings: Leo worked for Sullivan Printers, a business that
handled all printing jobs for Boston College, so he pulled for Jack
to choose the home team, fearing he'd lose his job otherwise, or,
conversely, receive a promotion if he convinced his son to attend;
and Coach Lou Little's representatives from Columbia reportedly
promised Leo a job if Jack attended school there, though the details
of this arrangement were less than clear.) Thus, though the time
Jack spent on the field was ultimately small, his consistently high
scoring statistics drew attention from the town, the local media,
college coaches and scouts, and, of course, girls.

Though darkly handsome, and a star athlete, Jack was nonetheless typical in his teenage shyness and self-consciousness around
the opposite sex. Until this point in his life, his sexual experiences
were limited to autoeroticism, which led to feelings of shame for
giving in to his intense sexual urges. Often more comfortable with
his boyhood friends, Jack became withdrawn and stoic around
girls. One contributing factor, Jack's full-blown Madonna/Whore
complex regarding women, clearly complicated matters
throughout his life; as biographer Dennis McNally pointed out,
"Rather than becoming either a prude or a degenerate ... Jack ...
hung suspended between the ethical boundaries, fascinated by the
perverse as well as the holy, unable to wholly commit himself to
either, and ultimately tolerant of both" (McNally, 11). Indeed, it
was this pull between different poles of desire that led Jack into a
puppy love triangle involving two very different girls: Mary
Carney and Peggy Coffey.

On New Year's Eve during his senior year, 1938, Jack went to a dance and met an Irish, redheaded girl named Mary—tall and thin, and viewed by other boys as somewhat gawky, she was called "Stretch" by Jack's classmates. She flirted and danced with Jack, and while she didn't intellectually challenge him—she hadn't gone further in school than junior high—he liked her nurturing, motherly aura; he spent the next few months going to her house in the evenings after track practice and dinner. And though Mary had had to initiate the first kiss, they later had marathon "make out" sessions while they sat at her family's kitchen table; Jack burned to do more but was quelled by his perception of Mary as a "good girl."

Soon, the two teenagers learned they had very different ideas about the future. While Jack dreamed of being a writer and leaving Lowell, Mary wanted to stay in the town, marry, and raise children. And while Jack considered sacrificing his dreams for hers, he nonetheless, meanwhile, sought out another, less "nice" girl to fulfill his sexual needs more completely.

Peggy Coffey, though also a tall redhead, was in many ways Mary's opposite; outgoing and brash, Peggy, a baton twirler, dreamed of being a band singer, thus providing a window into the world of jazz and swing that was beginning to draw in Kerouac. Reportedly, neither Jack nor Peggy took their dating too seriously, but he enjoyed Peggy's popularity and worldliness, something small town Mary would likely never have. Despite her deficiencies, however, Mary eventually received a proposal from Jack; she turned him down, telling him that he wasn't ready, and she urged him to learn a trade or work as a brakeman for the railroad. And while he waited for Mary to change her mind, Jack reconsidered his scholarship options, such that when Mary finally wanted him to propose again, he hedged, having come to embrace more fully the idea of going to college.

Upset, Mary started flirting with and dating other boys, and this sealed Jack's decision to leave the town of Lowell behind him. This was easier said than done, of course; Jack wondered throughout his life what would have happened had he stayed and made things work with Mary; he even wrote a book, *Maggie Cassidy*, about this particular phase of his life, demonstrating that he still ruminated on, and wondered about, the different path he would be on had he married her. But at the time, reeling from her so-called "unfaithfulness"—never mind that he had dated Peggy and Mary simultaneously—Jack became enamored with the idea of Columbia University and New York City.

So he made his choice. As a result, Leo did, in fact, lose his job and began to travel to find work (whether Jack knew this likely outcome of his college choice, regarding his father's professional life, is unclear), while Jack packed, borrowed bus fare from a family friend, and prepared for his first foray into the wide world outside Lowell.

CHAPTER TWO

Jack and the Beats Talk

Jack felt he was blasting so high that he was experiencing real insights and facing real fears.
—Ann Charters, *Kerouac: A Biography*

BEFORE KEROUAC COULD ATTEND Columbia proper, though, he had to attend school for one year at Horace Mann, a Columbia University's Teachers' College's training ground for fledgling teachers. Though experimental, it was nonetheless an expensive New York prep school that, in Kerouac's case, strove to fill the intellectual gaps left by Lowell's educational system, thus preparing him more effectively for the demands and rigors of an ivy-league school. He received a full scholarship for the year, and Gabrielle arranged for Kerouac to live with her stepmother in Brooklyn, forcing Kerouac to take a twenty mile, two hour subway ride every morning in order to reach the school in the Bronx. And once he finally got there each day, he didn't exactly feel at home. The students by and large came from well-to-do Manhattan families, a sharp contrast to Kerouac's penurious, blue collar background; and many of the students were Jewish, a group he had had no contact with previously, and about whom he'd heard nothing but negative things (Gabrielle and her stepmother were regular listeners of Father Caughlin's famous anti-semitic radio

rants). In spite of this, however, Jack made friends at Horace
Mann, writing other students' English essays for two dollars a
piece and going to jazz clubs (like the Harlem Apollo, the Golden
Gate Club, Kelly's Stable, and the Savoy Ballroom) with classmates
to hear the likes of the Count Basie Orchestra.

As McNally noted, this put Kerouac in an interesting position
regarding race relations. At the time he moved to New York, a
jazz club in Greenwich Village had become, just one year earlier,
the first integrated club in the country. Though Kerouac had
been a longtime music fan, records by black musicians had been
hard to find at this time. The American economy hadn't yet
found its feet, few records were released, and those that were
released were nearly by all white swing bands. But as Kerouac
became exposed to more and more African American musicians
and forms of speech, he became one of those truly American
enigmas: a racist who worships minority, specifically black, culture, condescending to it by making assumptions about its
inherent spirituality, exotic nature, and joyful simplicity. Indeed,
in *On the Road*, there is a famous, much-discussed passage
wherein Kerouac highlights this contradiction within himself,
arguably without much self-awareness:

At lilac evening I walked with every muscle aching among the
lights of 27th and Welton in the Denver colored section, wishing I
were a Negro, feeling that the best the white world had offered was
not enough ecstasy for me, not enough life, joy, kicks, darkness,
music, not enough night.... I wished I were a Denver Mexican, or
even a poor overworked Jap, anything but what I was so drearily, a
"white man" disillusioned. All my life I'd had white ambitions; that
was why I'd abandoned a good [Mexican] woman like Terry in the
San Joaquin Valley. I passed the dark porches of Mexican and
Negro homes; soft voices were there, occasionally the dusky knee
of some sensual gal; and dark faces of the men behind rose arbors.
Little children sat like sages in ancient rocking chairs. A gang of
colored women came by, and one of the young ones detached herself from motherlike elders and came to me fast—"Hello,
Joe!"—and suddenly saw it wasn't Joe, and ran back, blushing. I

wished I were Joe. I was only myself, Sal Paradise, sad, strolling in this violet dark, this unbearably sweet night, wishing I could exchange worlds with the happy, true-hearted, ecstatic Negroes of America.

Here, Kerouac exposes the envy he feels toward minority communities and expresses his lacking sense of identity as an American white man (a feeling with which many young people appear to empathize, as evidenced by the preponderance of hip hop culture among teens in all-white suburbs). Reportedly, Kerouac had a clear preference for black prostitutes during his first years in New York; had an affair with not only Terry, "The Mexican Girl" in *On the Road*, but also a Mexican prostitute (about which he wrote *Tristessa*); and later, he had a love affair with a black woman named Alene Lee (about which he wrote the novel, *The Subterraneans*). Thus, Kerouac's writing consistently reveals a dual attraction and condescension to those he considers exotic or "other," and passages such as this one clearly demonstrate an intense, deeply rooted self-loathing.

One friend of Kerouac's at Horace Mann, a British boy named Seymour Wyse (a/k/a Lionel Smart in *Vanity of Duluoz, Maggie Cassidy,* and *Visions of Cody*), introduced him to the saxophone players Charlie Parker and Lester Young, both of whom had a huge impact on the young writer. He began to look down his nose at the mainstream, dance-oriented, whitebread jazz of Goodman and Miller and argue for the purity of improvised jazz that disregarded entertainment as the goal and lauded, instead, expression. As noted by Amburn, "African American culture became the archetype of the loneliness and alienation of modern man, a central theme of Beat philosophy and writing" (47). Indeed, the improvisational phrasing and unfettered playfulness of this music, in large part, specifically inspired Kerouac's distinct writing style years later.

At the time he was a student, though, Kerouac started reporting on the New York jazz music scene for the *Horace Mann Record*, interviewing such luminaries as Count Basie and Glenn Miller. This struck his fellow students as passing strange. Columbia athletes with shaky academic credentials got funneled through the school fairly regularly, but they didn't normally perform so well academically (Kerouac maintained an eighty-two average), contribute work to the school's literary magazine, or write thoughtful articles in the school paper. Additionally, Kerouac performed well on the football field during this year, leading Horace Mann to victory enough times to establish the team as the unofficial champ of the city's prep schools.

Also during this time, of course, Kerouac explored different parts of the city, visiting museums, seeing French films in Times Square, and observing junkies and prostitutes who were living on the fringes of American society. One fall day, Kerouac pooled all the money he had saved and lost his virginity with a hooker, a memory he would later recall with affection. That winter, however, the world stage, seen by Americans through newsreels, evoked a bleak future, one that made a large scale war appear imminent, while political paranoia regarding radicals of any stripe swept through the country.

Despite this tense political climate, however, young, still-optimistic Kerouac asked Mary Carney to come to New York for the spring formal. They had seen each other when Kerouac came home for Thanksgiving and Christmas—in fact, in *Maggie Cassidy*, Kerouac reports that Mary asked him to make love to her during this Christmas break, but he refused, not wanting to "ruin" her—but by the time the dance came around, he felt wholly at home in New York. Though Mary surely fantasized about the glamour of this night, the reality was that Kerouac fit in, to some extent, among the places and people—sporting a white tie and tails—while Mary, in her simple, plain dress, felt horribly out of place, gauche, and self-conscious. At the end of the night, she begged Kerouac to return to Lowell with her, but he refused, sending her home in tears.

Kerouac completed his studies shortly thereafter, in the spring of 1940, but he was relegated to listening to Horace Mann's graduation ceremonies while lying in the grass behind the gymnasium, reading Walt Whitman. Though well-accomplished in school and sports, Kerouac was still nonetheless poor, and thus couldn't afford the clothes necessary (a white suit) to take part in the graduation exercises. Immediately after the ceremony concluded, Kerouac said farewell to his teachers and boarded a train bound for Lowell; there, he planned to do the work for the two courses he failed—chemistry and, ironically, French—but he never did, distracted all summer by Sammy Sampas and others in the Young Prometheans group.

Sammy and Kerouac became closer than ever over the course of this summer, with Sammy—with a cigarette holder in hand and a cape awkwardly fashioned from an old overcoat—acting as a kind of muse or literary mentor, urging Kerouac to read not only more Whitman but, additionally, Emily Dickinson, Thomas Hardy, and Jack London. Whitman seemed to affect both of them the most, though, convincing them of the wonder of small things in nature while also lauding America—the land as well as its democracy—and the hard-working common man; this led Sammy and Kerouac to define their political ideologies more sharply, thus supporting the system or party that appeared to champion the oft-romanticized downtrodden. (This was the only time in Kerouac's life that he aligned himself, or even flirted, with the left, though even then, the fiercely patriotic Kerouac couldn't get past his skepticism about what he viewed as the "Moscow-led" Communist Party in America.)

And not surprisingly, at one point during that summer, in a time when Americans heard speculation about an imminent Nazi invasion, as well as the horrors of the recent blitzkrieg, Sammy reportedly turned to Kerouac and said, "Don't think me insane, but I know, I *know* that I shall die young." No less dramatic than this prognosis was Kerouac's summer love life. He pursued a chaste relationship with Mary Carney once again while also sleeping with Peggy Coffey, whom his friends all thought was much better suited to him. Biographer Miles reported, too, that Ginsberg believed that Kerouac and Sammy had a kind of romance of their own, albeit a platonic one: "I think he thought of Sampas as being homosexually in love with him, he had a sort of crush on him, and Jack was in love with Sebastian," Ginsberg said (27).

No matter what amorous complications and confusions existed, however, come September, Kerouac caught a ride with friends and headed back to New York to start his academic and athletic career at Columbia University, moving into a dorm room on campus. He wore a blue and white beanie at all times, as was required of all freshmen, and washed dishes in the student union to earn his room and board. In his classes, he struggled with chemistry again, but Mark Van Doren's Shakespeare class inspired and excited him. On the football field—having sat out as wingback for the first half of his first game—Kerouac got the opportunity to start in the second game and suffered an injury. Doctors initially indicated that the injury was a sprain, from which he should recover quickly, so Kerouac went on training on what he thought was a problematic ankle, partly as a result of Coach Lou Little's needling (he suspected that Kerouac exaggerated the pain and was just being lazy).

Soon, however, x-rays revealed that Kerouac had a hairline fracture in his tibia; his leg was immediately set in a cast, relegating him to crutches, and his football season came to an abrupt end. Not that Kerouac didn't enjoy the perks of being injured; the Lion's Den, a gathering place for Columbia students, became Kerouac's home away from home, and he ate steaks and hot fudge sundaes by the fireplace there often while his leg healed. He read books and forgot about the job he'd been assigned as dishwasher in the dining room cafeteria. His class attendance grew spotty, and although he earned an "A" from Van Doren, he failed chemistry again. Despite this, his morale, generally, was up; Sammy visited him now and then, his leg seemed to be healing, and with many juniors and seniors leaving to fight in the war, his chances at being a starter during the next football season skyrocketed.

However, he returned to Lowell to find the town changed by world events; many of his friends were gone, serving their country, and instead of the old shawled Greek women who had previously inhabited the streets, prostitutes haunted the dark corners of the town. In an apparent attempt to re-claim an idealized past, Kerouac began to date Mary Carney again, and he learned to hitchhike to and from Boston—only twenty-five miles away—with Sammy. In terms of literary pursuits, Jack and Sammy shifted their attention that summer from Walt Whitman to Thomas Wolfe, spending hours reading and discussing the author's work.

Gabrielle and Leo, meanwhile, grumbled about Jack's failure to contribute anything to the family finances, but other than imparting a sense of guilt, their complaints had no affect on the young man's actions. At summer's end, when Leo had found a job as a Linotype operator in West Haven, Connecticut, Jack helped his parents move their possessions—first to a depressing, awful apartment that Gabrielle hated, then to a cottage by the ocean. The move made Kerouac uneasy, because he intimately associated his personal identity with the town of Lowell, and his parents' relocation thus left him feeling rootless and lost as he rode back to Columbia.

Things went from bad to worse, though, after Kerouac arrived in New York City; first, it was hard to concentrate on school subjects when the world's problems appeared to be hurtling America into a full-scale war, but then came news that shook Kerouac much more personally: he would not be starting in the first game of the football season. Though some biographies report that Kerouac had a heated argument with Lou Little, and others state that Kerouac just quietly packed his stuff and said that he was going to his grandmother's house, the end result was the same: Kerouac boarded a Greyhound and headed for Washington, D.C., for no other reason than because it was in the direction of Thomas Wolfe's hometown in North Carolina. He stayed one day, visiting the Capitol, the National Gallery, and the FBI and Department of Justice buildings, hoping to spot a famous politician; he watched a movie called *Dive Bomber*, during which he felt lonely and wept; and he wrote a letter to Sammy, from a cheap hotel room, that explained how out of fear and shame, Kerouac felt as though he couldn't go back to either his parents or Columbia. On such limited funds, however, he had to go somewhere fast.

The next morning, he sought out a bookstore and bought a book of Emerson's essays to read, essays that preached nonconformity and self-reliance; in this way, Kerouac's first yearnings toward Beat philosophies were taking root, though he still had a long way to go. He was too scared to hitchhike at this point, for example, and lacked the resourcefulness to strike out on his own, so he shamefacedly returned to his parents' home—a trend that would continue throughout his life, thus casting doubt on the legitimacy of his own "self-reliance"—and explained to them again, over their baffled, angry protests, that he wanted to be a writer. Meanwhile, in response to Kerouac's sudden, unexplained disappearance from Columbia, a New York newspaper soon obliquely reported that Kerouac would not be available for the upcoming football season, citing no further explanation for his absence.

Having sought out a job for the first time in his life, Kerouac quit a position in New Haven's rubber plant after one morning of work. Soon, he got another job, through a friend, as a gas pumper in Hartford. Renting a room, he spent his evenings developing short stories that were modeled after those of his favorite writers, Saroyan and Hemingway (a collection that would eventually be published, though posthumously, as *Atop the Underwood*). Sammy showed up unannounced on Thanksgiving day, urging Kerouac to return to Lowell and work at the *Sun*, the local newspaper, as a sportswriter for Charlie, Sammy's brother; and by coincidence, shortly thereafter, Leo wrote his son to tell him that he and Gabrielle were moving back to Lowell, so Jack happily followed and moved back home with his parents. But one Sunday, after seeing and being deeply affected by *Citizen Kane*, Jack came home to learn that the Japanese had attacked Pearl Harbor, thus throwing everything, including his daydreams, off course.

Kerouac enlisted in the Navy and waited to be called up while writing sports articles at the *Lowell Sun*; often, working efficiently if not carefully, he would file his story by noon, then spend the afternoon typing and working on his own literary projects. In the evenings, Jack worked out, talked with Sammy, read H. G. Wells novels, and occasionally slept with his old high school flame Peggy Coffey. While Leo loudly bemoaned his son's logic-defying choices, and World War II had sucked America into its conflict, Kerouac grew more introspective and self-absorbed, reading *Faust*, the book of Job, and everything Dostoyevsky wrote, with a keenly focused eye on the issue of fate and free will.

Soon, in this context, Kerouac's job at the *Sun* seemed silly and pointless; he began writing the first draft of *Vanity of Duluoz* on company time, after he finished his assignments. When he finally got fired for missing a scheduled interview, he headed down to Washington D.C. again, where GJ Apostolakis promised him a place to crash and a job working construction on the Pentagon building. And while the job came through, the appointment was short-lived; Kerouac was terminated for wandering around Virginia streets while on the clock. After being seduced by a waitress with a deck of pornographic cards, though, he temporarily moved in with her, letting her support him as he drifted. He worked briefly as a short order cook and soda jerk, but then eventually headed back to Lowell, fighting with his parents about his choices and feeling as though he barely recognized himself anymore. With this perspective, he wrote an apologetic letter to Coach Lou Little, and arrangements were soon made for Kerouac's return to Columbia. However, because he had failed his chemistry class, he would temporarily lose his scholarship, and he would need four hundred dollars to cover his costs until it could be re-instated. Kerouac was at a loss about how to raise the necessary funds until he talked with a merchant seaman one night in a Lowell bar.

Both he and Sammy decided to go to Boston, get passports and the necessary documentation, and see the world by serving their country—though Kerouac ended up going to the port city alone, for reasons that are unclear. Bizarrely, after his arrival, Kerouac was, in a single day, sworn in at a U.S. Marine Recruiting Center, and—after finding himself on the street again, restless and without guidance or direction—signed up next for the Coast Guard, having been fingerprinted and photographed at both offices. Suddenly panicked by his senseless behavior, and released into the city once again, he got drunk and passed out, spending the night in a Boston bar's men's room. Waking up, hung over and covered in his own (and other men's) filth, he decided to go to the National Maritime Union and beg for work. After spending several days at the Union Hall, Kerouac finally found work as a kitchen scullion on the *SS Dorchester*.

The boat left July 18, 1942, bound for Greenland, carrying a thousand construction workers, dynamite, and industrial

equipment, and although Kerouac was primarily drawn by the
job's money and the potential material for his writing, he also had
a sense that he was fulfilling a patriotic duty. Even this, however,
was tempered and made complicated by his sympathies for the
Germans; indeed, when the *Dorchester* lowered a depth charge in
the dangerous North Atlantic, destroying a German U-Boat, Kerouac did not celebrate with his shipmates but rather felt sadness
for the loss of "sweet blond German Billy Budd[s]" (Amburn, 63).
Amazingly, Kerouac's view in this regard held fast, despite the fact
that his own boat was attacked by torpedoes from a German U-
boat twice during the trip; also, on a more personal level, Kerouac
was reportedly sodomized on the ship by a "lecherous fatso cook
who deflowered" him (Miles, 33).

All this "adventure" proved too much for Kerouac, who, after
the crew safely landed on the coast of Nova Scotia, got feverishly
drunk on a bar tour and enjoyed a night of raucous exploits with a
hooker. This hedonism marathon unfortunately bled into a second
day, for which he did not have permission; the military police
soon picked him up, and he was fined for going AWOL in a foreign port. (In retrospect, however, Kerouac's high anxiety had been
well-founded. The *Dorchester* was torpedoed and sunk on its next
trip out, and many kitchen workers Kerouac had known
drowned.)

That October, Kerouac returned to New York to find that
Coach Lou Little had made the necessary arrangements for Kerouac's return and re-instatement at Columbia. But as always,
problems quickly arose. First, Leo came up for a visit and cornered
Lou Little in his office, complaining about the job that had been
promised him as part of Jack's recruitment package but never
materialized, as well as Jack's status on the team as a bench-
warmer. This, of course, didn't help Jack's case with Little. Second,
as Jack began working out with the team in practices, he focused
on an upcoming game scheduled with Army, a team who had a
player by the name of Henry Mazur. Mazur had played on
Lowell's high school team as a senior when Kerouac was a
freshman, and tradition called for seniors to have access to the
showers first, at all times; Kerouac tried to enter when the seniors

were showering, and Mazur harshly threw him out, embarrassing him in front of the whole team. For this reason, Kerouac couldn't wait to face his old nemesis and return the favor, but Little refused to play Kerouac in the game. This, along with Kerouac's decision that he had a future as a writer, not as a football player, led him to quit the team yet again. It would be the final time.

This put Kerouac at a crossroads again. But one of Kerouac's friends from Horace Mann, a French boy named Henri Cru (who also worked as a merchant marine), inadvertantly determined the direction that Kerouac would next proceed. One night, in between trips, Cru met a wild-spirited, attractive, seventeen year old art student named Edith "Edie" Parker, a woman who would act as a catalyst in first bringing together many of the artists who would come to compose the Beat Generation.

Hailing from Grosse Pointe, Michigan, an affluent WASP suburb of Detroit, Edie Parker came to New York in 1941 to live with her grandmother and pursue a career in art, having convinced her divorced parents to let her come. However, once in New York, Edie recoiled at her new high school's racial integration, so she started hanging out at the West End Bar, near Columbia's campus, rather than attending her classes. (Interestingly, most Kerouac biographies make a point of declaring Edie sexually adventurous but not promiscuous, noting that although she was sexually active, she normally remained faithful to one man at a time—with the exception of the time during which Kerouac entered the picture, crowding out his friend Henri.)

Cru and Parker had begun an affair following their very first meeting, but at the same time, Cru had decided to make his career as a merchant seaman, so he needed to get a job on another boat soon; he worried about leaving Edie, though, so he tried to think of who he could ask to keep an eye on her while he was gone. To this end, in January 1943, he brought Edie to Kerouac's dorm room so that they could meet and go to lunch. Apparently a terrible choice for a chaperone, Kerouac was smitten with Edie right away, sending her a hand-delivered love note the next day; Henri left, and Edie and Kerouac were almost immediately sneaking into her grandmother's apartment to make love on a red velvet couch. After only a couple of weeks, though, when things still hadn't seemed emotionally serious between them, Kerouac quit school and headed back to Lowell, unaware that Edie had gotten pregnant.

Edie, alone and unsure of who the father was (though she later insisted that the child was Kerouac's), confessed her indiscretion to her grandmother and arranged for an abortion. Though she told no one else about it then, it's clear that Edie did, eventually, tell Kerouac about the pregnancy, though the timing of this admission is a matter of some debate; some biographers place the conversation in the time just before Kerouac shipped out again later on the *SS Thomas Paine*, arguing that Edie, worried for Kerouac and wanting him to be careful, decided to tell Kerouac about her abortion at that time; others, however, argue that she told him months after he returned from that trip, when they visited her parents in Grosse Pointe, Michigan. Regardless of the timing, however, Kerouac's heated response is in no way a point of contention: he was furious. All reports agree that he yelled and raged at Edie, but obviously, there was nothing he could do.

To all appearances, he eventually forgave her, particularly since he couldn't even ascertain the child's paternity with any kind of scientific accuracy. (Indeed, Amburn posits that given Kerouac's response to and complete denial regarding a child he likely later fathered by another woman, Joan Haverty, Edie's instincts had been right; she knew perfectly well that although he would be furious about the abortion, Jack would be a billion times more incensed if she'd actually *had* the child.)

Thus, wholly oblivious to Edie's travails, Kerouac began working in earnest on a novel about his adventures at sea, called *The Sea is My Brother*, back in Lowell, showing the manuscript to an old professor at Columbia when he completed a draft. In March, however, the Navy finally called. Kerouac had wanted to train as a pilot in the Naval Air Force V-12 program, but he was rejected for officer training, though the reasons for this appear murky; according to Amburn, Kerouac failed a mechanical aptitude test; Miles, meanwhile, claims that Kerouac failed the medical examination; Nicosia argues that both factors contributed to the decision, explaining that Kerouac had suffered from German measles shortly before the examination, and that ultimately "he failed the physical because of a deviated septum, and he had difficulty computing altitudes as well" (103). Whatever the cause, Kerouac was subsequently shipped off to Newport, Rhode Island for boot camp.

Though biographers generally paint a bleak picture of Kerouac's brief time in the service, recently published letters from Jack to his mother, Gabrielle, seem to indicate that at least initially, he enjoyed and appreciated certain aspects of military life; fairly soon, however, the complaints about service life far outweighed the praise: the other, mostly younger men in the military bored him and couldn't offer him much in the way of stimulating, intelligent conversation; he couldn't sleep in the hammocks; the dentists on the base were hacks; and he had to deal with the indignity of washing garbage containers. Not surprisingly, given his behavior with the football program at Columbia, Kerouac soon found he couldn't live within the Navy's boundaries of strict discipline and hierarchy. One morning, tired of dull hours of drill and calling people "sir," Kerouac stood with a cigarette in his mouth during inspection, though cigarettes were strictly forbidden before breakfast. The commanding officer slapped the cigarette from Kerouac's mouth, and in response, Kerouac punched him, laid down his rifle, and walked toward the base library to spend the day reading, as he had in school years before. Military policemen soon arrived and hauled Kerouac off to the base sickbay for psychological testing. If found sane, Kerouac was informed, he would face a court-martial.

First, doctors physically examined Kerouac, then read through his novel manuscript-in-progress to gauge the workings of his mind. Also, Amburn reported, a crucial letter from Sammy Sampas, dated May 26, 1943, arrived at this time for Kerouac.

In his letter, Sammy rejected Western material and scientific progress as empty Faustian vanity and stated that personal ambition, the mainstay of American life, was pitiful. Western civilization had gone as far as it could and was now at a dead end. Most contemporary writers were spiritually bankrupt.... The

United States of America was ready to give birth to "a new soul," and modern life was about to change for the better. Finally, in an extraordinary presentiment of Kerouac, the Beat Generation, and the counterculture that followed it in the sixties, Sammy defined the new cultural paradigm: a noble savage, "crude, raw, unfinished," would rise from the devastation of World War II and mold the future, destroying old forms and creating a freer civilization. In the new order, people would connect with the Emersonian Oversoul, values would shift from rugged individualism to compassionate concern for one's fellow beings, and people would move from the crowded cities and rediscover the wide open spaces. As society would gradually renew itself, spirituality would flourish as never before, and art, "livingly created" in a revitalized vernacular, would be reclaimed from the academicians and given back to the common man. (72)

After sending this, Sammy left for the bloody fray of the war, but in this letter, we see that in addition to Kerouac's instinctive restlessness and interest in Emerson's ideals, Sammy provided Kerouac with what, in retrospect, seems a basic outline and recipe for Beat philosophy. Of course, the evolution and execution of these ideas lay in the distant future, and at the time, Kerouac had enough to worry about in his hospitalized state.

Leo came to visit his son, for once pleased and openly proud of him; convinced that Jack was sane, Leo thought his son was simply rebelling, in his own strange way, against fighting a war that neither Leo, nor his son (he assumed), supported. After making remarks about the "Marxist Communist Jews" who were behind the whole enterprise, Leo took a train back to Lowell, leaving Jack to consider his next move—one that would guarantee him a section eight discharge rather than a court-martial. On a Saturday morning, when recruits always lined the drill field and visiting Navy brass conducted inspections, Kerouac ran out from the hospital, naked, yelling "Geronimo!" He had also befriended a six foot, five inch former Louisiana State football player he called Big Slim, and together, they planned a hospital breakout, but they were caught before they could put it into action. Soon diagnosed with dementia praecox, better known now as schizophrenia, Kerouac was sent on to a psychiatric hospital in Bethesda, Maryland, where his co-conspirator Big Slim was headed as well.

In Bethesda, the patients were generally in much worse shape than they had been in Newport, many of them howling like coyotes. Kerouac tried to make the doctors understand that he wasn't dangerous, but rather that he was too independent to live within the military's rules, calling himself a "coward intellectual" and claiming himself to be "old Samuel Johnson." Finally, after several weeks, the Navy honorably discharged Kerouac in May or June 1943 (accounts conflict regarding the date) as a person of "indifferent character," though biographer Tom Clark noted: "Unofficially, the verdict of authority was that this Jean-Louis Kerouac was one cog that would fit in nobody's wheel. The machinery had ejected him" (56). Troubled by his failure to serve his country, Kerouac made his way back to his parents then, though they now lived somewhere new: an apartment above a drugstore in Ozone Park, Long Island.

It wasn't Lowell, but Gabrielle had brought Jack's green desk and other belongings, making it as much like his original home as she could. Gabrielle and Leo, meanwhile, were getting along better than they ever had before; Leo worked as a Linotype operator at a Canal Street print shop, and Gabrielle worked on a skiving machine in Brooklyn, making military footwear. With both kids grown and (usually) out of the house, the couple had finally come into a substantially easier life than they had had previously, financially speaking. They even went out on Saturday nights to eat in Manhattan restaurants and see Broadway shows; it was like a second courtship, and both were happy. During this time, Jack exchanged letters with Sammy Sampas, who was fighting overseas, and sought out his old flame Edie Parker. She was in Asbury Park with her grandmother for the summer, so he hitchhiked there, and she welcomed him back into her life and bed.

Before Edie had come to Asbury for the summer, though, she shared an apartment on 119th St., near Columbia's campus, with a woman named Joan Vollmer Adams. Joan was married, but her husband, who had been a Columbia student, was off fighting in the war. Well-read, intelligent, and sarcastic, Joan, a journalism student, was a good roommate match (and, reportedly, sexual mentor) for Edie. Edie had finally broken things off with Henri Cru—telling him of her affair with his friend—and had dated others in the meantime, but when Kerouac arrived at her doorstep, they picked right up where they left off. In August, Joan moved to an apartment on 118th Street, but this time, the lease had the signatures of Joan, Edie, and Kerouac (who falsely signed as a married couple), the latter of whom was scheduled to ship out again soon for two months.

For despite Kerouac's unsavory experiences on the *SS Dorchester*, he signed up for another trip and boarded the *SS George Weems*, a boat that transported bombs to Liverpool. He largely isolated himself from the other crewmen and worked on his novel *The Sea is My Brother* on the purser's typewriter every chance he got. And in the spirit of his journey to Britain, he brought books of English literature along—specifically, John Galsworthy's *Forsyte Saga*. This, in part, reportedly inspired the idea of Kerouac's *Duluoz Legend*, whereby all his works could be interconnected, and thus presented as one continuous work. But this is not to say that Kerouac always had his head in the clouds while on board the ship. On watch one night, he spotted a mine that would have otherwise sunk the ship. And he had undergone a change since his time on the *SS Dorchester*; according to Nicosia, a German submarine attacked the ship one morning, and upon hearing this, Kerouac simply turned over in his bunk and went back to sleep. He and the crew did survive, of course, but after arriving in Liverpool, Kerouac attended a classical music concert at Royal Albert Hall, got drunk, sought out a prostitute for the night, and then employed another the next day. Eventually, he stumbled back to the ship in the dark of a blackout. (Though he may have responded differently to the threat of danger, he still responded in the same ways to express his relief and happiness in surviving.)

And although the boat was attacked by Germans again on its return trip, the crew eventually made it back to Manhattan safely. Edie was glad to see Kerouac, but her concern for him had, at its lowest point, turned into anger at his abandonment, an act which fueled her to duplicate Kerouac's first love letter to her and sell copies for one dollar each; the buyers were primarily servicemen who wanted to make girls swoon, and it was an effective enough letter that it earned Edie approximately fifty dollars total. Nonetheless, Edie forgave Kerouac upon seeing him again, and he soon became a fixture in her and Joan's apartment. He eventually took Edie to Ozone Park to meet his parents, and although they didn't dislike her, Gabrielle was upset by Jack's plan to live "in sin," so Jack tried to commute back and forth between his mother's house and Edie's apartment. Not surprisingly, though, the bulk of his nights were spent in the city, reading aloud Joyce's *Finnegan's Wake* with Edie, making love, getting drunk, and tentatively discussing marriage. Edie spent her days, meanwhile, working as a longshoreman during this time, operating forklifts in order to load mattresses for soldiers onto ships.

Also at this time, Edie had begun spending time with Lucien Carr, a stylish, handsome, sophisticated young man in her drawing class at Columbia. Like Edie, Lucien came from some money— hailing from St. Louis and tenuously linked, by marriage, to the Rockefellers—and despite initially feeling jealous and threatened by him, Kerouac ultimately found himself drawn to the worldly, engaging, blond-haired charmer as well. (Charters reported that Carr was even more impetuous than Kerouac, which was no small feat; on the night they first got drunk together, Carr told Kerouac to get into an empty barrel, which he did, and Carr rolled it along the Broadway sidewalk.) Indeed, nobody seems to have been able to resist the magnetism of Lucien Carr, but this seductive power had, in addition to social advantages, some dark consequences, in the form of a tall, red-haired, bearded, thirty-three year old admirer named David Kammerer.

Formerly Lucien Carr's scoutmaster in St. Louis, Kammerer had been so obsessed with the boy that he had followed Carr to Andover, Massachusetts, then Brunswick, Maine, then Chicago (when Carr attended the University of Chicago), and then finally to New York, moving his life repeatedly and working menial jobs in order to stay near the object of his desire. (Originally a physical education teacher at Washington University, Kammerer was working as a janitor in Greenwich Village when Kerouac met him.) Biographers believe that Carr's resemblance to a boy in Paris with whom Kammerer had had a previous affair was the reason for his erotic fixation. Miles explained, though, that Kammerer didn't fulfill a "typical stalker" profile. He was friends with Carr, and although Kammerer demanded the young man's time and attention, he generally controlled himself and didn't force himself on Carr physically. The situation nonetheless got to be too much sometimes, as witnessed by Carr's suicide attempt (via gas inhalation) in Chicago. Reportedly, the two could normally be friendly because Kammerer's sense of humor amused Carr, while the attention obviously fed Carr's ego and made him feel important.

At one time, Kammerer had been business partners with Carr's father, who, after leaving the family to be a shepherd in Wyoming, had died years before. (The family fortune stemmed from Carr's maternal grandfather, who dealt in jute and hemp fibers, among other things.) Indeed, Kammerer's link to the Carr family had once been strong enough to convince Lucien's mother to allow her son, then fourteen years old, to accompany Kammerer on a trip to Mexico. There, Kammerer made his first sexual advances toward Lucien, who, not surprisingly, felt lost and utterly confused, leading to his first experiences with alcohol.

During the Christmas holidays of 1943, when most Columbia students had left campus for break, Carr met yet another man who would fall in love with him. One night, while Carr listened to the stereo in his room, a seventeen year old Jewish boy with big ears knocked on his room door, inquiring about the music. In this manner, Carr became acquainted with Allen Ginsberg, a young freshman at Columbia. The son of a socialist father, who was a teacher and a published poet, and a Russian communist schizophrenic mother, who was in and out of psychiatric hospitals, Ginsberg had had a home life and a childhood in Paterson, New Jersey that were vastly different than most. The bounds of what Ginsberg considered "normal" behavior were thus significantly broad. Already aware of his homosexuality at age seventeen, Ginsberg, a closeted virgin, fell in with the extroverted Carr easily, developing a crush on him that would cause his career interests to shift from becoming a labor organizer to an aesthete—one who was most interested in philosophy and literature (though Ginsberg's political leanings guided his public life as a poet and ultimately resulted in a life path that consistently combined both passions). It was Ginsberg and Carr who first hatched the idea of creating what they called a "New Vision," or "post-human post-intelligence," inspired as they both were by French symbolist poets and Fyodor Dostoyevsky, who they discussed for hours on end. This "New Vision" gave name to the expression of their feeling of restlessness, and the frustration of the suffocating restraints they felt were artistically oppressive. The "New Vision," they felt, would offer the opportunity to overcome these social and intellectual hindrances and make art that had more immediacy, and thus more visceral impact.

Additionally, Carr soon told Ginsberg about his friend, Jack Kerouac. Curious about this sea-faring athlete who was also a writer, Ginsberg showed up at Edie and Kerouac's apartment one day at noon, in the spring of 1944, unannounced. Reportedly, Kerouac had just gotten up and was sitting in an armchair when Ginsberg looked him in the eye and said, in a serious tone, "Discretion is the better part of valor." Kerouac, unshaken and unimpressed, said something along the lines of, "Aw, shut up, you little twitch," and then called to Edie, loudly inquiring about his breakfast eggs.

Despite the rocky start, however, a friendship developed between the two men; according to Ginsberg, they went walking after breakfast, discussing Dostoyevsky, among other topics, and by Ginsberg's report (from an unpublished lecture), they felt an intellectual affinity for one another: "[Kerouac] told me how when he was in Lowell, Massachusetts, he used to stand in the back yards at night when everybody was eating supper and realize that everyone was a ghost eating ghost food. Or sometimes that he was a ghost, watching the living people" (Miles, 50). This constant, hyper-awareness of mortality and the fleeting nature of human existence not only linked the two men, but revealed, early on, the source of Kerouac's terror: the feeling of invisibility, a haunting version of living death.

Yet another person who appears to have loosely followed Carr's circuitous path, though less threateningly and deliberately than Kammerer, was another well-to-do young man from St. Louis named William Burroughs. Kammerer was Burroughs' friend and had introduced him to Carr in Chicago, where the boy attended school while Burroughs worked as a bug exterminator. Burroughs later followed Carr (and, of course, Kammerer) to New York, where Carr would attend Columbia and Burroughs would study psychology, undergo psychoanalysis, and work as a bartender. Burroughs, whose grandfather founded the Burroughs Corporation and invented the adding machine, had a sharp intellect and an impressive education, having studied anthropology and literature at Harvard, psychology at Columbia, and medicine in Vienna. A gay man who didn't, at first, discuss his sexuality openly, and older than most of the Beats by about a decade, Burroughs was to became a crucial mentor in Kerouac's development as an artist, though Burroughs didn't at the time foster writing dreams of his own, as did Carr and Jack. (And not unlike many of the other Beats, Burroughs had some mental health issues, having, in one case, sliced off the end joint of a pinky finger as a VanGogh-esque declaration of love to a man who was no longer interested.)

Kerouac and Burroughs' first meeting, not surprisingly, was cautious and strange. In the spring, after Burroughs had heard Carr, Ginsberg, and Kammerer prattle on about this footballer-turned-author who looked like a movie star, he showed up at Kerouac's doorstep uninvited, Kammerer in tow. Dressed in his usual neat, formal manner—Brooks Brothers seersucker suit, a homburg, and a chesterfield—Burroughs studied Kerouac, who was just out of the shower, with great interest and curiosity. Kammerer provided the pretense for the visit, saying that it was a fact-finding mission about getting work as a merchant marine (in which Burroughs was supposedly interested), but Kerouac had the clear sense that Burroughs just wanted to see, and meet, him in person. Self-conscious about Burroughs' lascivious looks at his half-naked, still-steaming-from-the-shower athletic body, Kerouac was nonetheless flattered and intrigued by Burroughs' intellect and distinct, eccentric mannerisms. As Kerouac would later describe Burroughs at this meeting, in *Vanity of Duluoz*,

> Tall, 6 foot 1, strange, inscrutable because ordinary-looking (scrutable), like a shy bank clerk with a patrician thinlipped cold bluelipped face, blue eyes saying nothing behind steel rims and glass, sandy hair, a little wispy, a little of the wistful German Nazi youth as his soft hair fluffles in the breeze.

Thus, at that moment, another part of the Beat picture fell into place, and the artists who would play an enormous role in the evolution of movements within the arenas of politics, literature, film, philosophy, religion, fashion, sex, and drugs (among others), for the next several decades, were first brought together. And for a brief period, they had the time of their lives, challenging and playing off each other for hours at a stretch.

In March, 1944, though, shortly after his twenty-second birthday, Kerouac learned that his dear old friend from Lowell, Sammy Sampas, had died in the war. He had been wounded at Anzio beachhead, north of Naples, Italy, and was transported, by ship, to Algeria, where he lay in his hospital bed and asked for a recording machine, with which he recorded poetry-filled messages for both his family and Kerouac. Jack wrote a grief-stricken letter, half in English and half in joual, addressed to Sammy, and also exchanged maudlin, tragically sad letters with Sammy's sister Stella, who had always had a crush on Jack. These last letters demonstrate not only Kerouac's deep sadness, but also his anger. In his opinion, the United States had no business fighting the Nazis; this was a Jewish war, and was simply about money, which wasn't worth losing lives over, in his opinion. But nothing could bring Sammy back, and in some ways, Ginsberg and Burroughs, together, stepped into the role that Sampas previously filled in Kerouac's life as a literary mentor.

Later that spring, in 1944, Kerouac accompanied Edie to Grosse Pointe, Michigan, to meet her parents, but he left her there in May to seek out work on a ship back in New York. Not finding a job, he impulsively headed to New Orleans to look there. Still unsuccessful, he stopped off in Asheville, North Carolina, to visit the homeland of Thomas Wolfe—meeting and getting drunk with the author's brother, reportedly—then arrived back in New York, much to Edie's joy. This unstructured, random trip was a harbinger of the restlessness that would soon take hold of Kerouac, but his ties to home, particularly his mother, still always drew him back, causing him to suggest to Edie that after they married, they should live with his parents in Ozone Park. (To her credit, Edie was, not surprisingly, never on board with this idea.)

At this time, a kind of literary salon formed among Kerouac and his friends. Carr—who Kerouac noted early in their acquaintance was much more engaging in person, and in conversation, than he was ever going to be on the page—was fascinated by a concept he learned of called actes gratuites: i.e., committing an action without motivation or reason. In one instance, when the group was gathered, as they often were, at Burroughs' place for dinner, Carr grabbed the steak that Burroughs had intended to share among the group and began to chew on it. Kerouac and Burroughs, unfazed, watched as Carr began to growl like a tiger, and then Kammerer joined in, playfully struggling to wrench the steak from Carr's hands. Similarly, on another night, Carr noticed a small tear in Burroughs jacket sleeve. He stuck his finger in it, making it grow into a hole, and Kammerer grabbed at the other sleeve, yanking it completely off the jacket. Kammerer then tied the freed sleeve around Burroughs head—while the staid intellectual hardly reacted at all—and the two men continued tearing at the jacket, draping strips of material across Burroughs' bookcases and lamps. Though most likely baffled—a blue collar boy observing the decadent destruction of another person's property— Kerouac was nonetheless riveted by Carr and his behavior, and the friends seemed to relish each other's spontaneity and challenges to convention. But only a few months later, in the middle of August, everything drastically changed.

Tension had escalated between Carr and Kammerer, with the former claiming that the latter would come into his room at night and stand in the darkness to watch Carr sleep. And because Carr spent so much time with Kerouac, Kammerer, in a fit of jealous rage, went to Jack and Edie's apartment once with Burroughs and, finding the place empty, tried to hang Kerouac's kitten with a tie (fortunately, Burroughs stepped in and saved it, deciding not to tell Kerouac about the incident for some time, fearing what he would do). Carr, who was involved and in love with a beautiful, French Barnard student named Celine Young, grew impatient with the melodrama that always seemed to surround him.

Late at night on August 13, 1944, after he and Kerouac almost got work assignments on a ship (they immediately got thrown off by a surly first mate who was embroiled in a union dispute), Carr sat in the West End Bar and listened to Kammerer plead with him to go for a walk. At three a.m., they strolled out into the hot night to Riverside Park to have more drinks; there, reportedly (though the facts of the event are anything but clearly established), Kammerer—at wit's end, having recently threatened Young and told her he would kill himself soon—apparently tried to rape Carr, telling him that he would kill Carr if he refused to have sex. Carr grabbed his pocketknife, stabbed Kammerer twice, in the heart, and then panicked. He bound Kammerer's hands and ankles together with shoelaces and tried to strap rocks onto Kammerer's body in order to sink it into the Hudson River. The rocks weren't heavy enough, though, and Kammerer floated up to the water's surface. Flustered, Carr undressed, walked out into the water, and gave the corpse a shove, but as it moved down the river, Kammerer's feet bobbed horribly, hauntingly on the water's surface.

Watching this, Carr got dressed again, his clothes covered in Kammerer's blood, and made his way out of the park to the street, where he hailed a cab. Catching one, he gave the driver the address of Burroughs' apartment in Greenwich Village, so that he could tell his friend what had happened. Burroughs advised Carr to go home, immediately contact a lawyer through his mother, and plead self-defense, arguing that Kammerer tried to rape him (thus making it an "honor slaying," according to one New York newspaper of the time). Instead of doing that, however, Carr went to Kerouac and Edie's apartment next. Kerouac, still asleep in the early morning, listened as Carr said, "I just got rid of the old man." Kerouac sent Edie, who hadn't understood the statement, to the kitchen to make them breakfast, and Carr asked Kerouac to take a walk with him. During the course of their extended stroll around Manhattan, Carr dropped his pocket knife (the murder weapon) into a sewer grating, and he buried Kammerer's glasses in a park while Kerouac created a diversion for passersby. From there, they went to a bar to drink, then to the movies, watching *Four Feathers*. They ate hot dogs in Times Square, visited the Museum of Modern Art, and went to yet another bar. Finally, after all this, Carr found the courage to turn himself in, and the two men parted. Quietly, as if it were any other day, Kerouac took the subway uptown to the apartment he shared with Edie.

But Carr's cooperation with the police didn't get Kerouac off the hook; by helping Carr dispose of and hide evidence, Kerouac became at best a material witness, at worst an accessory. (Burroughs had been arrested as a material witness also, but his family immediately bailed him out, taking him back to St. Louis for the week until Carr's arraignment occurred.) Arrested and sent to the Bronx City Jail—nicknamed the "Opera House" because of its inhabitants' tendency to "sing," or rat out friends and/or co-conspirators—Kerouac read works by W. Somerset Maugham, Aldous Huxley, and Nikolai Gogol. Leo, embarrassed and infuriated that a son of his would be involved in a murder scandal (especially one that involved homosexuals), refused to help Jack, leaving him to turn, shamefacedly, to Edie.

He promised to marry her—which he soon did, getting a temporary release to go to City Hall and meet his bride and the Justice of the Peace; his guard was best man and witness. After celebrating for a while in a local bar—the kindhearted prison guard reportedly bought everyone drinks—Kerouac headed back to prison, though Edie soon got the money for his bail from her family. Carr, meanwhile, pled manslaughter and was sentenced to the highly ambiguous term of one to twenty years in a reformatory (because of the crime's portrayal as an 'honor slaying' wherein Carr was defending himself, the judge sympathetically granted him what could potentially be an easy stint, served in an environment far less severe than a state prison).

The newly free Kerouac went with Edie to Grosse Pointe,

working to re-pay the bail money he owed to her family. Edie worked as a riveter for Chrysler, while Kerouac counted ball bearings on the factory's night shift; but he was restless, uncomfortable, and unhappy. He and Edie cheated on each other, and within two months, he claimed he wanted to sail again as a merchant marine, so Edie's father arranged for him to go back to New York to catch a ship. He signed up, but while waiting for it, he stayed in Ginsberg's dorm room and tried hard to seduce Celine Young, Lucien Carr's beautiful former girlfriend; though Kerouac was still married to Edie, defaulting on his commitment was not what bothered him about the situation. No, what Kerouac felt most guilty about, strangely, was the fact that Young had been Carr's girlfriend, and his culpability on this point—his apparent betrayal of Carr—continued to sting, resonate, and fester in his mind for years, as demonstrated by the appearance of this seemingly small event again and again in letters, journals, and other writings.

Soon, though, he boarded the SS *Robert Treat Paine*, getting a job, despite his inexperience, because of the shortage of eligible seamen. One crew member noticed Kerouac's incompetence regarding ship operations early on and began to taunt him, calling him "handsome," "pretty boy," and "sweetie-pie." Consequently, Kerouac, feeling sexually harassed and fearful of what would happen to him at sea again, shoved his seaman's uniform into his duffel and jumped ship at the first port of call; in response, the Maritime Union blacklisted him for one year.

With his tail between his legs, to some extent, having failed to serve yet again, Kerouac sought out Ginsberg and shared his Columbia dorm room in secret, not telling Gabrielle and Leo, Edie, or anyone else, for a time, that he was in New York and not at sea. (One exception to this, apparently, was Celine Young, whom Kerouac tried to seduce again.) But despite Kerouac's attempts at a hidden, simple life, a complication arose: Ginsberg not only admitted, for the first time, that he was a homosexual, but he also told Kerouac, during one of their many all-night talks, that he loved him. Kerouac, who seemed primarily worried about how this admission would affect their friendship, groaned. He appeared not to reciprocate Ginsberg's romantic interest, (though Ginsberg claimed that there was, at various later times, sexual interaction between the two men.) During this period, however, Kerouac appears only to have maintained a strong friendship with Ginsberg. After Kerouac found his own room, Ginsberg retrieved and chose library books for him. Kerouac also adopted an artistic course of what he called "Self-Ultimacy," whereby he burned everything he wrote (to prove that it was pure art), and bled onto a small card labeled "the blood of the poet," which he tacked onto the wall. He met with Ginsberg twice a week to talk, get drunk, and exchange books, but he otherwise worked hard writing in isolation until Burroughs came back to town and said, in one of his wiser, more sober moments, "My God, Jack, stop this nonsense and let's go out and have a drink" (McNally, 74). From then on, though Kerouac still thought about, discussed, and worked toward this "New Vision" that he, Ginsberg, Carr, and Burroughs sought, he stopped setting himself apart from the world.

Nonetheless, Kerouac was the root of many problems that Ginsberg began to have at Columbia. A bartender reported Ginsberg's consistent late night drinking bouts to a dean, who ordered Ginsberg to live in an on-campus dorm; there, Ginsberg wrote shocking obscenities on his windows (i.e., "[the dean] has no balls," and "Fuck the Jews") to vex the unpleasant, Irish cleaning woman who had failed to clean the windows for months, and a dean walked in one morning to find Ginsberg in bed with Kerouac; while the exact nature of this cohabitation (sexual or platonic) has been disputed among biographers, the end result was the same: Ginsberg, for the moment expelled, found a room on West 92nd Street, and Kerouac moved into Burroughs' apartment, where he began working, jokingly at first, on a collaborative novel about the Kammerer incident with Burroughs (the much-fabled, never published *And the Hippos Were Boiled in Their Tanks*, written in the hard-boiled style of Dash Hammett).

Not surprisingly, Burroughs became at this time a huge influence on Kerouac, urging him toward morphine use, as well as toward the work of philosopher Oswald Spengler, whose work caused Kerouac not only to long for the "simple life"—achieved through communing with nature and surviving by way of resources primarily provided by the outdoors—but also to have a romanticized image of native cultures and third world peoples. Similarly, Burroughs encouraged Kerouac to read LF Celine, a stream-of-consciousness writer who used ellipses (...) between thoughts instead of more conventional punctuation breaks—thus anticipating Kerouac's use of the endash between thoughts in his own future works—and used vernacular French, demonstrating to Kerouac that authors could indeed presume a certain amount of license and break away from rigid stylistic rules.

One project Kerouac worked on during this time was a novella, originally titled *The Half Jester,* which became *Orpheus Emerged;* the story focuses on a group of earnest young intellectuals who struggle with existential questions, as well as with the problems that arise when trying to apply, and thus force, ideological theory onto one's lived, real life and behavior. The book, which wasn't published until 2000, thirty-one years after Kerouac's death, shows a writer's awkward beginnings; the big ideas are there, as are the figures drawn from his life, but the prose is stilted, and the execution pretentious, demonstrating clearly that Kerouac had not yet found the energetic, frenzied, musical voice that would become his artistic trademark.

After working on these projects, Kerouac returned to Joan and Edie's apartment in January 1945 and attempted to reconcile with his wife. Joan, now with a baby daughter, Julie, and newly separated from her husband, needed money, so she soon rented out other rooms in the apartment to Burroughs and Ginsberg. (Unexpectedly, Burroughs and Vollmer became lovers and soon married, despite Burroughs clear sexual preference for men.) At this time, while so many Beats central to the movement were gathered in a single living space, other individuals who would figure large in the scene appeared. A large, red-headed prostitute who used the alias Vickie Russell, for instance, introduced Kerouac and his friends to Benzadrine during this time, showing them how to take blotter strips (which were soaked in the drug) out of nasal inhalers, roll them up, and swallow them down with coffee or Coke. These were called "speedballs," and the user was hopped up with energy for hours, though the crash that inevitably followed was, by all reports, harsh and unpleasant. (Kerouac and the other Beats, most notably Joan, would abuse this drug for years, with collectively awful results.)

Another important figure, who reportedly introduced the term "Beat" as Kerouac would soon apply it to his friends and himself, was a perpetually strung-out bisexual con man named Herbert Huncke. A friend of Burroughs—who was permanently fixated on the low-life fringe element of American society—Huncke introduced Burroughs to morphine (to which he would spend his long life addicted) and commonly used the term "beat" to mean "exhausted." Kerouac soon associated Huncke, and those like him, with the word "beat," such that it came to represent the disenfranchised and disillusioned people in America: those who didn't neatly fit into the system and who tragically strove, at all costs, to be true to themselves, their needs, and their desires.

As Amburn pointed out, Kerouac sought examples in the realm of contemporary artists to illustrate the concept more clearly: "Montgomery Clift's famous slouch was Beat, as were Dane Clark's tortured Dostoyevskian intensity and Brooklyn accent, Charlie Parker's black turtleneck sweater, John Garfield's portraits of battle-hardened, sardonic servicemen, and Marlon Brando's conga drums. As Marlon Brando wrote ... 'It was ecstasy sleeping on the sidewalk of Washington Square, realizing I had no commitments to anything or anyone'" (96). The term "Beat," as it evolved in Kerouac's mind, also eventually took on spiritual weight, such that "Beat" also assumed a relationship to "beatitudes," referencing the blessings that Christ handed down during his Sermon on the Mount.

No amount of blessings or good fortune could save Kerouac's marriage, however. At the beginning of summer that year, Kerouac moved back to Ozone Park to stay with his parents. Edie returned to the Detroit area to arrange for an annulment, and her parents were shocked at their daughter's condition; she and Kerouac had been so poor that they primarily fed themselves mayonnaise sandwiches, and Edie's Benzadrine use had taken its toll upon her wasted, gaunt form as well. But of course, nearly all the members of this artistic community became addicted to drugs, to varying degrees, and the group began to unravel and shift when the war finally ended in August, 1945. (Upon the return of Joan Vollmer Adams' husband from the war, he found the stoned group in her apartment and asked, incredulously, a question along the lines of, "This is what I fought for?") Edie had left the 118th Street apartment, and Hal Chase, who had served in the army as a ski trooper, entered the scene and moved in, pursuing affairs with both Celine Young and Burroughs. Hailing from Colorado, and thus embodying the American West for Kerouac, Chase was a handsome lady killer whom Kerouac monopolized and wanted to emulate. But Chase's arrival nearly coincided with the initial failure of Kerouac's father Leo's health; it was Banti's disease, or cancer of the stomach, so advanced as to be inoperable. And although Leo had been far from a perfect father and husband, his impending death shook Kerouac, who from grief drew a new sense of drive and ambition regarding the creation of his art.

He stayed up nights, writing while hopped up on Benzadrine. The drug helped his morale, as he felt strong and confident while high, and the fact that he could take such huge doses was, to him, a measure of his toughness and masculinity. Not surprisingly, though, Kerouac's Benzadrine addiction caught up with him, and in December, after getting started on a new novel, he collapsed and had to be hospitalized. Diagnosed with thrombophlebitis, Kerouac had developed large blood clots in his legs, a condition that could have been fatal had the clots spread to his brain. When Jack came home from the hospital for two weeks to recover, he found himself confronted by the constant image of his ailing father. Jack listened while his father groaned and cried from pain every two weeks, when the doctor came to drain fluids from Leo's stomach, and while he asked Jack to promise to always to take care of Gabrielle. Jack accepted and took this oath seriously, and though he often got drunk and rambunctious with his ornery father during this time, he knew Leo was suffering terribly.

Finally, in the spring of 1946, Leo died. Gabrielle, stoically, performed her spring cleaning and then returned to her job in a shoe factory. Jack, miserable with guilt and remorse, disentangled himself from his friends—whom his parents and he had come to blame for his downfall—and worked more feverishly on the project that would become *The Town and The City*, hoping to make his father proud. The sprawling, epic novel focused on the Irish-Catholic Martin family, and although the young characters were largely based on Jack, Nin, and Gerard, and the parents were modeled after Gabrielle and Leo, critics and biographers have long noted that the family depicted seems to have more in common with the Sampas family than the Kerouacs.

At this time, though Kerouac occasionally checked back in at Joan's 115th Street apartment, to re-fuel his system with marijuana, Benzadrine, and liquor, he primarily lived and worked in Gabrielle's house, working odd jobs. This defection coincided with a general disbanding of the Beats which occurred during this year. Joan was temporarily institutionalized in Bellevue because of her severe addictions, and when she was released, Burroughs moved with her to Texas, planning to grow and sell marijuana there; Ginsberg stayed, more often than not, with his parents in New Jersey during this time; and Huncke, the hustler who appeared to have unintentionally given the group their name, landed in the Bronx jail. A time of upheaval and change was clearly upon them all.

But near the end of this year, a man Hal Chase knew from home, in Colorado, came for a visit; his name was Neal Cassady, and his presence among the Beats seemed to provide them with the final, missing, "New Vision" puzzle piece.

■ CHAPTER ■ THREE

The Call of the Road

*Someone can wander from city to city, as Kerouac
was doing, if he has a strong sense of himself and
knows the reasons for his being in all those lonely
rooms and for riding on all those endless buses. But
Jack's desperate flights back and forth across the
country during the next six years only mirrored his
own confusion.*

—Ann Charters, *Kerouac: A Biography*

IN LOWELL, AT THE TENDER age of eight, Kerouac had once
attempted to travel beyond the familiar boundaries of his hometown, looking for kicks and adventures. With two friends, he
hiked nearly twenty miles toward Pelham, New Hampshire, but
after only one day, the boys, shivering and damp, were found near
the banks of the Merrimack and returned to their homes. This
failed attempt at travel not only demonstrated Kerouac's yearning
to explore different parts of the country at a young age but also
mirrored his first, not-so-glamorous nor well-strategized attempts,
as an adult, at "drifting."

The man who initially inspired Kerouac's urge to move from
place to place—twenty-year-old Neal Cassady—arrived in New York
with his pretty, sixteen-year-old, high school dropout cheerleader

wife, LuAnne Henderson. The two had traveled from Nebraska in a car Neal stole from LuAnne's uncle—though it broke down early on, and they had to catch buses the rest of the way—and lived, for a time, on the three hundred dollars that LuAnne stole from her aunt. (These relatives had helped them, providing the couple with a place to stay before Neal and LuAnne robbed them blind.) And although there appear to be different versions of how Kerouac first met Cassady—including a lustreless meeting in a bar, wherein Kerouac was less than impressed with the strident, antsy young man—the account most often offered in biographies mirrors the scene that opens *On the Road*: Kerouac comes to the coldwater flat in Harlem, where Cassady and LuAnne are staying; after Kerouac knocks on the door, Cassady opens the door, stark naked, while LuAnne, also nude, scrambles to dress in the background, making it unabashedly obvious that they had just been having sex.

Though the accuracy of this account as the two men's first meeting has been widely called into question, the incident would regardless be a fitting first impression for a man whose long, stream-of-consciousness style letters to Hal Chase—which Kerouac and Ginsberg had voraciously read—possessed to have an unprecedented electricity, energy, and spontaneity to them. Cassady had written these missives while cooped up in a New Mexico reformatory, sentenced there for theft. Despite deadbeat appearances, however, Neal had intelligence and cared about art and literature, carting around a volume of Shakespeare's works and a book of Proust among his meager earthly possessions, stuffed in a bag.

Born in 1926, in Salt Lake City, Utah, Cassady's parents had separated by the time he was six years old. His mother took the younger children with her while his father, an alcoholic, got full custody of Neal, so Cassady's early memories consist of sleeping on a bare mattress in a flophouse in Denver, going to a mission for a handout breakfast (where he was usually the only child around), and then, occasionally, heading off to school. Though he liked reading, and was thus a favorite among teachers, he was also strong, so other kids didn't pick on him. His father, meanwhile, provided him with training that would serve him well as an adult;

during the summers, the father and son would hitchhike or catch freight trains or boxcars, traveling to find work or family members. By the time Neal was a young teenager, he developed a penchant for hanging out in pool halls, in the poor section of any town, and stealing cars for the purpose of impressing girls—whom he charmed easily—and joyriding. By his own estimation, he co-opted five hundred cars between the years of 1940 and 1944, though he was only caught in the act three times.

Appropriately, if not ironically, Cassady sought a job parking cars once he settled in New York, and though he charmed most of the Beat set, a few kept their distance. Burroughs, for one, as well as Edie, Celine, and Joan, all sensed that Cassady was untrustworthy and a fake; in contrast, this new guy on the scene fascinated Kerouac, and the two men seemed to sense in each other what was lacking in themselves—in Cassady's case, a stable home and family and a good, formal education; in Kerouac's case, an unashamed, hedonistic enthusiasm and energy that didn't allow conventional boundaries or rules to dictate action and induce feelings of guilt or shame.

The real relationship of note at this time, however, evolved between Ginsberg and Cassady. Almost immediately, upon their first meeting, they developed an intense level of intimacy, leading to days upon days of marathon talking sessions (thus satisfying Neal's declared intellectual yearnings) as well as to a sexual relationship; in this way, Ginsberg monopolized Cassady's time (just as Kerouac had previously done with Carr and with Hal Chase), wanting this new addition to the Columbia crowd all to himself. Kerouac struggled to come to terms with this unexpected turn of events; he had always tended to deem Ginsberg's homosexuality as a weakness, whereas in Cassady, Kerouac appeared to view homosexual tendencies as liberating and brave. (Significantly, Kerouac did not categorize Neal as gay, but rather as "pleasure-seeking.")

Cassady's young wife LuAnne, lost in all of this new activity in New York, became increasingly upset about her husband's new obsessions and friends; for they left him little to no time to spend with her, so she lied to Cassady: to get his attention, she told him that cops had been by the apartment, asking about Cassady because of how much marijuana he had been buying. The plan backfired on LuAnne, however, since it merely scared Cassady from spending *any* time at the apartment; soon, a despondent LuAnne packed her bags and returned to Denver, in March, 1947. At this time, Cassady showed up on the Kerouacs' doorstep in Ozone Park, asking Kerouac to teach him how to write. Though Kerouac sensed immediately that this was simply a ploy by Cassady to hustle a place to stay temporarily, he nonetheless opened his home to Cassady, despite Gabrielle's reservations. (Though Jack knew better than to tell her about Cassady's stints in reform school, she nonetheless instinctively didn't trust Neal.) There, while Kerouac typed, working on *The Town and the City*, Cassady read Jack London's works aloud and watched over Kerouac's shoulder, cheering him on as he would a jazz soloist in a club.

It should be noted that in addition to Cassady's envy of Jack's talent, education, and family, another possible reason for Cassady's affinity with him—though less passionate than his kinship with Ginsberg—may stem from Jack's resemblance to Cassady's half-brother, also named Jack. Born of Cassady's mother's first marriage, Neal's half-brother had Native American blood and appeared to embody perfect masculinity to the impressionable young boy; he had encouraged Neal, for example, to throw darts at him and hit as close to his body as possible—like a knife-thrower—and when the darts hit his chest by accident, Jack dismissed it, forever impressing Neal with his physical toughness. Certainly, this kind of calm remove, seriousness, and athletic masculinity were also parts of Kerouac's persona, to which Cassady clearly responded.

However, not much time passed in Ozone Park before Cassady packed for Denver; Kerouac and Ginsberg accompanied him to the bus station to say goodbye. While there, the three posed for photos in a booth; Kerouac's picture reportedly made him look like a mobster, and Ginsberg and Cassady split it evenly down the middle, both wanting it for themselves (a moment recounted in *On the Road*). Ginsberg soon made plans to move out West to resume his affair with Cassady, and Kerouac became enchanted with the idea of traveling across the country as well. In the meantime, though, Kerouac received letters of his own from Cassady, one of which detailed his numerous, attempted seductions of girls on the Greyhounds that shunted their human cargo across the country. Kerouac noticed, while reading these letters, that Cassady felt no compunction to follow grammatical rules, writing freely without censor or a rigid sense of control. The style seemed to capture Cassady's voice and spirit in a way that startled Kerouac, thus providing him with the germinal seed of what he would later name, and make famous, "spontaneous prose," a style that he would adopt and use himself for the bulk of his career.

Ginsberg, who was anxious to be together with Cassady again—and jealously troubled by Cassady's talk of a new woman in his life named Carolyn Robinson—traveled to Denver in May, and Hal Chase, graduating early from Columbia, headed back home to the same city. Kerouac, jobless and working on his epic novel, had no income and saw no way to join his friends and see the country. He felt stuck.

After traveling to the South with Gabrielle to visit Nin and her new husband, Paul Blake (her first marriage ended in divorce), Kerouac returned to Ozone Park, dejected. At this time, Henri Cru, Kerouac's old friend from Horace Mann, appeared; he was on his way to San Francisco to catch a ship, on which he had a job as an electrician. Recognizing Kerouac's growing wanderlust, Cru suggested that his friend could likely get a job on the ship as well. Wanting to encourage her son to work, Gabrielle, supporting him still by way of her wages as a skiver, told Kerouac that he should go, and that she would help.

Excited, Kerouac reached what he approximated to be the halfway mark of his sprawling novel—about six hundred pages—and then made plans to start his cross-country journey at Provincetown, expecting to hitchhike along Route 6 all the way to Nevada. He got a ride to Provincetown, but then, while standing in the pouring rain for hours, he discovered that there was little to no traffic—certainly no transcontinental traffic—and gave up, finally catching a bus to New York City, and then another to Chicago. Similar to his failed attempt, at age eight, to strike out and see the world, this trip was not turning out the way he romantically imagined it would.

But after catching yet another bus to Joliet, to escape the congested gridlock of Chicago traffic, he finally began to travel as he had wanted and intended all along: catching free rides with strangers (mostly farmers and truckers), having adventures, and exchanging stories with everyday Americans. (Of course, as McNally notes, America, adjusting to life after the war, was just then in the throes of becoming what Kerouac despised: middle-class and suburban, a trend which entailed "social conformity, materialism, and a lock-step faith in 'scientific progress'" (95). He ate apple pie slices with ice cream often along the way, whenever the opportunity presented itself, considering this "meal" nutritious (?) and good-tasting, and when he finally reached Denver, he found Hal Chase at the Denver Art Museum, where he was continuing his anthropology studies. Kerouac soon learned, though, that two factions had formed among his Columbia friends in Colorado: Hal Chase's band of friends, and Cassady, who was with Ginsberg most of the time. Chase's set considered Cassady an untrustworthy bum, but regardless of this opinion's veracity, Cassady was a busy man at this time. He worked during the day, then tried to keep three lovers—LuAnne, Carolyn, and Ginsberg—happy and sexually satisfied.

As a result, Kerouac didn't see much of Cassady on this first trip (though he did meet Cassady's new mistress, Carolyn, with whom Kerouac shared a mutual attraction). Instead, he spent most of his time partying with Chase and his friends; one day, the group took over an old, abandoned Victorian house and invited everyone out in the street to join them for a party there. Such gatherings were essential to the development of the Beat movement and thus became the lifeblood, since they often spawned intellectual discussions, poetry readings, music performances, and sexual openness. As Amburn explained, "Without this coming together among the young, the culture of the isolated, dug-in middle class would have continued to dominate, and the social changes of the counterculture might never have come about" (118). But despite the fact that Kerouac was having the time of his life, he eventually, of course, had to wire Gabrielle for more money so that he could continue on to San Francisco.

Meanwhile, Cassady seemed to be distancing himself from LuAnne, and soon, he left with Ginsberg to drive to Burroughs' ranch in Texas. Carolyn, a graduate theater student, calmly took Cassady's desertion in stride: she packed for Los Angeles to pursue a career in costume design. Once again, everyone seemed to be breaking apart, and when Kerouac reached Henri Cru in California, he found out that unfortunately, there was no job for him on a ship. Instead, he and Cru got jobs as night watchmen for barracks that housed construction workers who traveled overseas to jobs. Kerouac, given his distaste for, and distrust of, authority, didn't like the job, thinking that his co-workers assumed the role of "cop" too happily. But he liked the regular paycheck, which he usually forwarded on to Gabrielle, and he and Cru often broke the rules by eating their fill each night in the camp's kitchen, as Kerouac described in *On the Road*; this practice eventually got them fired, but in the meantime, Cru convinced Kerouac to try his hand at screenwriting. After Kerouac pounded out a script, Cru approached studios with the screenplay in hand, but not surprisingly, no one was interested.

During this stint, Kerouac received letters that had traveled through the thick drug haze of Burroughs' ranch. Not only were Ginsberg and Cassady there, but also Huncke, William and Joan, and the children, Julia and Bill Jr. (a new addition to the family, though not a wholly happy one; because Joan didn't even cut down, let alone stop, her drug use during her pregnancy—on average, taking two hits of Benzadrine a day—the infant was born with withdrawal symptoms, causing him to cry and scream nearly constantly). Descriptions of the Burroughs' ranch at this time evoke a haunting, nightmarish netherworld of the type imagined by the artist Hieronymous Bosch:

> Burroughs was doing three shots of heroin a day, and Joan was perpetually wired on Benzadrine. Huncke's legs were covered with boils, and his body was full of holes from repeated jabbing with heroin needles. Little Julie was now four years old and had a

disturbing habit of gnawing her arm, which was covered with scars. No one bathed her, and Joan permitted the child to defecate in the Revereware, the same pots she used for cooking. (Amburn, 121)

Thus, although the people at Burroughs' ranch likely felt that they were promoting, and working toward, a new, enlightened way of living, the reality was that their extreme self-absorption exposed the dark side of this new perspective—revealed when taken to such extremes—and hinted at the pain and destruction that would soon lie in its wake.

Ginsberg, however, who seemed to exert more self-control than the others regarding drug use, noticed that during his stay at the ranch, Cassady was pulling away from him, and this nearly drove Ginsberg to a mental breakdown until Cassady, in September, finally told his lover that their relationship was over. Ginsberg, heartbroken, arranged for a position for himself on a ship that was scheduled to depart soon, and Cassady promised to spend one last night with him; however, when Neal traveled with Ginsberg and Huncke to Houston, he took off in the car after drinking and getting high with them in a bar; Ginsberg waited in the darkness of night while Huncke entertained a young man in their hotel room. When Cassady finally returned, he loudly burst into Huncke's room with a woman on his arm. Everyone grew agitated and fought until Cassady passed out, not waking again until late morning. Hurt yet again, Ginsberg missed his freighter that morning, but he left the following week to work on a ship headed to West Africa.

Kerouac, meanwhile, also feeling the need to travel, caught a Greyhound to Los Angeles; in the bus station, he experienced a feeling that appears in *On the Road*, inspiring one of the most charming, wistful, and sympathetic passages in the book: "all of a sudden I saw the cutest little Mexican girl in slacks come cutting across my sight. She was in one of the buses that had just pulled in with a big sigh of airbrakes; it was discharging passengers for a rest stop.... I wished I was on her bus. A pain stabbed my heart, as it did everytime I saw a girl I loved who was going the opposite direction in this too-big world." The woman *did* end up stepping onto Kerouac's bus, though, after all, and while Cassady's reported erotic exploits may have initially triggered Kerouac's attempts at bus seduction, the end results were significantly different. Bea Franco (called "Terry" in *On the Road*), a migrant worker who was escaping an abusive husband, and who had a seven-year-old son staying with relatives, connected with Kerouac so intensely that by the time the two reached Los Angeles, they were making plans to hitchhike to New York together.

All told, they stayed together for a couple of weeks, at first in a cheap Hollywood hotel room, and then in a tent with Bea's son in Selma, where Kerouac worked hard picking cotton for a dollar and fifty cents a day—not even enough for food. Although Kerouac probably liked the *idea* of living this kind of "fellaheen" life, the reality wore on him as the nights grew cold in the tent, and he soon shipped Bea back to her family and caught his own bus to Los Angeles, and then Pittsburgh, where his money ran out. Two hitched rides got him to Harrisburg, Pennsylvania, where he slept on a bench in the railroad station, but the next day would prove equally trying: though he got a ride to New York, it happened to be with a lean man who believed in strict dieting, which struck the starving Kerouac as tragically funny. Hungry and exhausted, Kerouac had finally made it back, heading to Gabrielle's house in Ozone Park. There, his mother no longer made a fuss about Jack living off her savings and hard-earned wages, and she left him alone while he isolated himself from the outside world in order to finish his novel.

Working through the winter of 1947 and onward, visiting his New York friends only occasionally, Kerouac was suddenly shaken up in June 1948 by a troubling letter from Cassady. Suicidal, the twenty-two year old had plowed across stop-signed intersections, hoping to be hit; he had held a gun to his temple; and he had placed himself in circumstances wherein he hoped he would freeze to death in his car. (In tragically funny, typical Cassady-fashion, though, he grew impatient, as well as uncomfortably cold, and gave up, but his radiator had frozen by then; he flagged down a bus, which pushed his car to a gas station for repairs, and he was soon on the road again, as if the whole thing had never happened.)

But he was still alive, despite all efforts, with a pregnant mistress, Carolyn, and a wife, LuAnne, who would turn eighteen very soon, thus making annulment an exceedingly more difficult affair.

Thus inspired, Cassady had set out on a mad, marathon driving spree to Mexico, getting his marriage annulled just in time; he married Carolyn two or three days later. (Cassady told Kerouac that this child, though it was Carolyn's first, was the fifth that he had fathered.) After the wedding, the impending birth of the child seemed to re-invigorate Cassady, who hatched a plan then to develop a kind of commune: a ranch where all of their friends could live together out West. Kerouac latched onto this dream as well, stating in letters to Cassady that he could use the huge advances he would surely receive for the film rights to *The Town and the City* (though of course, such interest never materialized). In Kerouac's mind, this commune would encourage free coupling—men with women, women with women, men with men—and Gabrielle would do much of the work. He also envisioned an ideal wife for himself: a wild party-girl who would also be only too happy to see to the house's upkeep, as well as cook for him, the Cassadys, and any other drifter who might happen by. And although this plan never came to fruition, the ideal captured young people's imaginations in the sixties, spawning the growth of hippie communes, wherein the traditional, conventional yearnings of community and love were conjoined with the new Beat ideals of freedom and self-reliance.

While Kerouac precociously dreamed of this land-based, rural existence, though, Ginsberg and Burroughs had returned to the bright lights of fast-paced New York, soon taking Kerouac to parties, jazz clubs, and gallery openings. During the course of these cultural events, Kerouac met a young writer named John Clellon Holmes, who, though four years younger than Jack, seemed older by virtue of his stable marriage and maturity. The two men grew close, having long talks about literature and music (Holmes was a fan of dixieland, while Kerouac introduced him to improvisational bop), and in September, Kerouac finished the first completed draft of *The Town and the City*, which was a whopping 1,183 pages in length. Ginsberg was the first to read the manuscript, which he praised and pushed onto two of his former professors (Mark Van Doren and Lionel Trilling). Scribner's—Thomas Wolfe's publisher—quickly rejected the novel, the first of many rejections that Kerouac would receive for his work. And while these initial setbacks stung Kerouac, he nonetheless began work on two other projects that would evolve into *Dr. Sax* and *On the Road.*

On the other side of the country, meanwhile, Cassady worked for the railroad and struggled to write a memoir titled *The First Third*; Carolyn thought he'd finally settled down, but by the end of 1948, she had learned otherwise. Neal, after being laid off in December, took the couple's savings and bought a car (without consulting Carolyn, of course), announcing that he would drive to North Carolina, where the Kerouacs were celebrating the holidays at Nin's house; Neal, ostensibly, planned to bring Kerouac back with him to California. Hitting the road with two friends, Al and Helen Hinkle—in addition to LuAnne, whom he woke in Denver at three in the morning to convince her to come along, despite her engagement to a shipped-out sailor—Cassady drove dangerously fast across the country, as usual. (For this reason, Helen opted out early on along the way, in Tucson, heading for Burroughs' farm in Texas with the intention of meeting up with Al there later.)

Arriving just as Christmas dinner made its way to the Blakes' table—utterly baffling Nin and the others—Cassady, LuAnne, and Hinkle nonetheless pulled up chairs to share in the feast. Cassady, perhaps to get himself into Gabrielle's good graces, impulsively offered to help her move some furniture and other items back to Ozone Park, so he, Kerouac, LuAnne, and Hinkle soon hit the road again, accompanying Gabrielle's strapped-down possessions. After unloading them into the house, they returned to Nin's home in Rocky Mount to collect Gabrielle herself and drive her back to Ozone Park, too, covering more than two thousand miles, remarkably, in only three days.

After their labors, though, the group partied hard, ringing in the new year (1949) for three weeks before packing back into Cassady's Hudson for another cross-country trek. The first part of their journey took them to Algiers, Louisiana, where the Burroughs' were now living. Burroughs, who had never been impressed by Cassady, wrote a letter to Ginsberg that expressed wonder at Neal and Jack's aimlessness:

> Neal is, of course, the very soul of this voyage into pure, abstract, meaningless motion. He is the mover, compulsive, dedicated, ready to sacrifice family, friends, even his very car itself to the necessity of moving from one place to another. Wife and child may starve, friends exist only to exploit for gas money. Neal must move. (Charters, 109)

Burroughs had no idea how prescient, and accurate, these words would be, particularly after the crew made their way to California again. But to get started, Helen, Neal, Jack, and LuAnne left Hinkle and his wife behind and hit the road again, with little money but lots of confidence and optimism. To facilitate their trip, they pawned items, picked up hitchhikers, panhandled, and stole food, and despite the desperation of these acts, they successfully made it back to San Francisco. There, however, to Kerouac's surprise, Cassady did something that Kerouac never forgot, nor wholly forgave: Neal deserted him, leaving him penniless and homeless with LuAnne, while Neal sped off to be reunited with Carolyn and their little daughter, Cathleen.

LuAnne, hurt but resilient and resourceful, returned to a flea-bag hotel where she'd stayed previously and convinced the manager to give her and Kerouac a room on credit. The two made love for a couple of days, though LuAnne considered Jack distant as a lover. (Indeed, as in many aspects of Kerouac's life, he appeared simply to be making mental notes constantly, thus translating raw experience for the purpose of his writing rather than being more fully present in the action.) LuAnne quickly grew bored with the situation and, aware of her financial circumstances, began prostituting herself to make her way back to Denver. Appalled and disgusted by this, Kerouac again sought out Cassady, who this time offered him a place to stay in the apartment he had moved into with Carolyn. The two men frequented local jazz clubs for a few days, but then, after receiving money wired from Gabrielle, Kerouac made a circuitous bus journey—including a short visit to Grosse Pointe to see Edie—back to Ozone Park.

Nearly two months later, Kerouac received a letter of acceptance from Harcourt Brace for *The Town and the City*. With an advance of one thousand dollars, and an agreement to work on revisions with an editor (Robert Giroux), Kerouac made the deal. Re-ignited with confidence, Kerouac struggled with the beginnings of a novel he decided to call *On the Road* before deciding to head back to the west coast. Finding a cabin in Denver, where he settled in to write, he found all of his friends gone, leaving him depressed and lonely.

In New York, meanwhile, Ginsberg got into trouble with the law, having found himself being pulled over with Huncke and two others while in a stolen car. Though Ginsberg claimed to be riding along for the experience, so he could effectively write about it in a story, the excuse sounded laughably implausible and desperate. Nonetheless, because he wasn't involved in any criminal activities himself, he got off; but based on the content of his diaries and short stories, confiscated in the car, he was sent to a hospital for psychiatric evaluation. Kerouac sent Ginsberg letters during this time to cheer him up but was feeling desperately lonely himself, so he soon packed up his things and continued on to San Francisco, where he lived with Neal and Carolyn.

At that time Neal was, physically speaking, a mess. He had begun seeing LuAnne on the side again, and once, while fighting with her, he hit her and broke his thumb; he also needed leg surgery because of a cyst; had such severe foot problems that he had to see a podiatrist twice a week; had to take cough syrup nightly; and as a consequence of collapsed cartilage from a previous operation, he had to blow his nose constantly. Needless to say, Kerouac hadn't been prepared to find his young friend in this condition. But after spending some time partying together, and angering the oft-neglected Carolyn, the two men came across precisely the kind of deal that neither of them could pass up: a used car salesman offered them the chance to drive a '47 Cadillac limo to Chicago for a client. Needless to say, they jumped at the chance—without talking to newly-pregnant-again Carolyn, of course—and blew their way across the country in a startlingly short time, thanks to Cassady's combination of skill and recklessness in driving.

After delivering the limousine successfully (another anecdote recounted in *On the Road*), Cassady and Kerouac traveled by bus to see Edie Parker again in Grosse Pointe, where, after throwing parties and having a pleasant visit, she and Jack discussed how they would finally pursue, and follow up on, an amiable divorce from one another. Jack and Neal then caught a ride as passengers in a Chrysler headed to New York, making their way back to the city; this time, they landed in a rented house in Richmond Hill, Queens, where Gabrielle had recently moved. She still didn't trust Neal, though, and after three days, she made him leave. After he and Jack said goodbye, he struck out on his own in the city and soon began a relationship with model Diana Hansen—a woman he was still dating in January, 1950, when Carolyn gave birth to Jamie, another daughter.

Two months after Jack and Neal's return to New York, *The Town and the City* hit bookstores nationally, and although the reviews were generally neutral to positive, reviewers noted Thomas Wolfe's obvious influence on the writing, and the book quickly dropped from the literary world's radar. As Ann Charters noted, Kerouac's "talent as a writer was not his inventiveness with new characters and plots, but rather his power to dramatize the spirit of his own life into romantic fantasy" (66–67). For this reason, Kerouac's first novel felt flat, since he had simply gone through the motions of what he still thought, and had been told, fiction had to have and be. Nonetheless, Kerouac's hometown friends turned out for a book signing party in Lowell, and Kerouac's Denver friends scheduled a similar party. To attend, Kerouac traveled west only to find Cassady there, too, on the verge of traveling to Mexico for a no-fuss divorce, so he could cut Carolyn loose and marry Diana (who was five months pregnant with Cassady's child herself). Very likely, Kerouac would have been ready and willing to go along on the trip regardless, but Burroughs had recently moved to Mexico City after having more legal troubles in the States; thus, Jack probably didn't hesitate a moment to join Cassady and his friend Frank Jeffries on the road.

Mexico was a revelation to the men, particularly Kerouac; though he had felt sympathy for, and an understanding of, the romanticized "fellaheen," or dark-skinned peoples of economically poor countries, he had never before seen them up close. In one town, a young man who sold the men marijuana also told them that he could take them to a whorehouse, which the men availed themselves of for a generous length of time. Eventually, though, they moved on to Mexico City, where they rented an apartment next to the Burroughs' house. Jeffries signed up for acting courses; Kerouac got high and wrote furiously, reading the bible in fits and starts; and Cassady blew the money Diana Hansen gave to him—expressly for the purposes of attaining a divorce—on dope.

After going broke, Cassady headed back to Diana in New York to commit bigamy, and true to classic Cassady form, he headed back to California within an hour of marrying Hansen, citing his railroad job at San Luis Obispo as the reason, though he was on his way back to reconcile with Carolyn. (Hansen had written and typed a letter that Cassady sent Carolyn, urging her to begin divorce proceedings, but Cassady never received the papers or a response.) In spite of Carolyn's past experiences with Cassady and her heartbreak, and because she was pregnant again, she accepted him back into her life by year's end.

And while Cassady struggled to work his way back into the heart of his old love, Kerouac embarked on a wholly new amorous venture. The woman's name was Joan Haverty, and she was a twenty-year-old tall brunette from Poughkeepsie, New York. She had lived with Bill Cannastra, a wild, alcoholic, bisexual partyman—a friend of Ginsberg's, originally—who had died suddenly and tragically (decapitated while riding on the subway, after his body got stuck leaning out the window). After only knowing each other a couple of weeks, Haverty and Kerouac married; they hitchhiked upstate to visit her parents, then Haverty resumed her job at a department store while Kerouac worked on *On the Road*. The arrangement seemed temporarily ideal but was short-lived, since Kerouac yearned to live with Gabrielle again, wanting not only the company but the nurturing and care she provided him. Thus, the newlyweds made the bad-idea move to Gabrielle's rented house in Richmond Hill.

On December 17th, Kerouac received a letter from Cassady—a long missive that has since become known as the "Joan Anderson Letter"—that energetically and informally told the story of a few sexual conquests, as well as a Christmas weekend in Denver spent in flophouses, jails, and pool halls; Cassady had intended this piece for inclusion in an autobiographical novel he was struggling to write. Reportedly, Jack read the letter on his subway ride to work, and then re-read it for two hours later that same day; even Joan got caught up in the letter, such that dinner was delayed an hour that evening because of it. (Unfortunately, only fragments of the letter now survive; Ginsberg, upon hearing Kerouac rave about it, broke into Kerouac's place to procure it. What remains of the letter has been published in the back of Cassady's *The First Third*, published by City Lights.) Accounts as to the letter's length varied widely—13,000 words as well as at 40,000 words—but one thing remains constant: Kerouac insisted that it was the best thing he ever read in his life. Inspired by his friend's style, Kerouac re-dedicated himself to working toward a prose that was vivid and real, practicing, through the exchange of letters to his friend, what would become the style that would define not only *On the Road*, but Kerouac's work as a whole.

Fortunately for Joan, Gabrielle decided, in January 1951, that she would rather spend the cold winter with Nin in North Carolina, leaving Jack and his wife to move back to Manhattan. Haverty got a job as a waitress while Kerouac worked as a part-time script-reader and synopsis writer for Twentieth Century Fox—jobs that paid the bills. In the evenings, Joan spent much of her time as a seamstress while Jack continued to focus on his writing. It was at this time that John Clellon Holmes published his novel, *Go*, which centered on the Beat scene and included almost verbatim recounts of conversations that Holmes had had with Kerouac and his friends (though their names had been changed, as Kerouac also would always do in his own novels). Even though *Go!* suffered from a distant remove that undermined its subject—not surprising, since Holmes himself, though fascinated by the

Beats, never seemed a true part of the group—Kerouac's jealousy and bitterness-fueled marathon writing sessions, as did his consistent drug of choice, Benzadrine. Thus, Kerouac grew impatient with the smallest interruption to his long stints of constant typing, including having to stop to put more paper into the typewriter. To solve this "problem," he experimented with using rolls of drawing paper that measured twelve feet in length.

Kerouac also began work on another project, which would eventually become *Visions of Cody*. More experimental than the first *On the Road* misfires, in terms of form, Kerouac drew content again from the notebooks he kept during his travels. And while *Cody* would not be completed for some time—and not published until 1960—a nearly mythical three week, coffee-motivated writing jag ensued in April 1951, which resulted in the production of Kerouac's first completed manuscript of *On the Road*, written in a single paragraph on one continuous paper roll.

Significantly, during this time in Kerouac's artistic evolution, a friend named Ed White had suggested, while they dined in a Chinese restaurant, that Kerouac should work like a painter with words, or verbally "sketch." Taken with this idea, Kerouac, on his way home from the dinner, took out a notebook and described what he saw in a bakery window. In his view, this kind of writing resembled the transaction within a confessional, wherein holding anything back was a sin. And though he'd tried to write of his travels previously, he had approached the work this time as a means of telling Joan about his past adventures, and through these various tweakings regarding his process, something clicked. He seemed, finally, to achieve the style for which he had been searching, and he felt proud of his great accomplishment. But as he would soon learn, the world wasn't quite ready for his discovery.

CHAPTER FOUR

Finding a Voice

[T]he big mad capping final night of the great poetry reading with Allen on the stage before a hundred eager Raskolniks [sic] in glasses crowding in from the rear of the reading hall, with wine in my hands a gallon jug I'm drinking yelling "Go," Allen is howling his HOWL pome and other crazy poets there, it's mad, it will never end, I just wrote a huge letter to Burroughs about it .

—Jack Kerouac, *Selected Letters, 1940–1956)*

IRONICALLY, WHEN KEROUAC FINISHED the initial draft of *On the Road*, inspired by the desire to share the memories of his travels with Joan, his marriage began to fall apart. Kerouac had suffered, not surprisingly, from the depression that often follows frantically busy periods of work—a kind of post-partum sense of loss—while also possibly contending with substance withdrawal symptoms. To cheer himself, he spent time with old friends like Lucien Carr, often staying out all night; one night, though, he returned to the apartment he shared with Joan to find his neglected wife with a male co-worker. And while this angered him, it didn't compare to the rage he felt when Joan, after telling him that she was pregnant, refused to terminate the pregnancy. Having caught her in an affair,

74

Kerouac voiced fervent skepticism about the child's paternity and in June, he moved back into Gabrielle's home in Richmond Hill.

What Joan didn't know, of course, was that Kerouac himself had already become embroiled in an affair too by this time (making his moral indignation toward his wife a bit hypocritical). For Kerouac had taken up with a strikingly beautiful, exotic-looking young artist named Adele Morales, and they dated for the better part of a year (though she eventually moved on to marry another important writer of this generation, Norman Mailer). Professionally, though, Kerouac began to circulate his new *Road* manuscript in July, initially sending the roll of type to editors at publishing companies. Not surprisingly, editors were in turn intrigued and baffled by the strange package. Harcourt Brace rejected it immediately, so Kerouac sought out an agent and forwarded it elsewhere. Meanwhile, his health suffered again as a result of his benzadrine binges, forcing him back into the hospital for the month of August while he contended with further bouts of phlebitis.

Regarding his writing, however, Kerouac staunchly maintained that in order to retain the purity of his spontaneous prose, he should not, and would not, revise the original draft of his work. However, not only was this an awfully hard sell to publishers who were perplexed by the very nature of this new work, but Kerouac's biographers differ widely as to how true to this ideal Kerouac managed to be. For while many insist that he tweaked and tinkered with the *On the Road* manuscript for six years, others, like Amburn, argue that the version that finally made it into print is only different from the original scroll in the smallest ways (changing the names of real people to pseudonyms, punctuation, etc.).

In Kerouac's June 23, 1957, letter to John Clellon Holmes, he wrote that the bound book of *On the Road* was identical to the scroll. Then he confided his "secret," revealing that Viking was under the false impression that he had spent the past five years extensively re-writing the manuscript. On the contrary, he told Holmes, the bound book was the "shining original." ... My own feeling, from all Kerouac said to me about the handling of *On the Road*, was that he effectively resisted Cowley's editing, only to be ambushed later by Viking's copy department. (259–260)

Perhaps with the recent auction of Kerouac's original scroll, scholars can glean a more definitive answer as to the differences between the original and published versions of the book whose inception has become a publishing legend.

News from Kerouac's friends at this time in his life, however, was more clear-cut in nature. Cassady informed Kerouac of the birth of his third child with Carolyn, John Allen (named for Kerouac and Ginsberg), while the news from the Burroughs' family in Mexico was tragic: in the spirit of William Tell, a strung out, drunk Burroughs had tried to shoot a shot glass from his wife Joan's head; instead, however, the bullet struck her temple, killing her almost instantly. She was buried while Burroughs waited in a nearby jail cell to make bail. In this way, Joan became a warning symbol, the star of her own Beat Generation fable, and thus an example of the dangers inherent in the group's pleasure-seeking lifestyle.

Someone who only encouraged such addictions called to Kerouac like a Siren from the opposite coast at this critical time: Neal Cassady. Promising that Carolyn would take care of them both, he urged Kerouac to come out to California, and this invitation, paired with Henri Cru's encouragement to get a job on a ship with him, led Kerouac to pack up and, once again, head West. Arriving in Los Angeles in December, he met up with Cru, and although they drank and celebrated Christmas together, Cru failed yet again to retain a position for Kerouac on his ship. Unfazed, Kerouac traveled to San Francisco, where the Cassadys had already, in anticipation, made a space in their home for Jack. In the attic, Carolyn and Neal had put down a mattress, brought in a small desk, a radio, a clock, and a stack of books, thus creating a fully functional, albeit small, writing loft. For Kerouac, this was ideal; when he wanted company, he had only to come downstairs; when he wanted to work in privacy, he squirreled himself away in his garret; and when he wanted to go out, he could slip into the city to drink and listen to live music. For one of the only times of his life, Kerouac managed to strike just the right balance between his desire for both isolation and community, and for a time, he was happy and productive, typing for hours at a time up in his attic nest.

Not that there weren't problems. One significant occurrence that nearly all of Kerouac's biographers note is that during this time, on Cassady's birthday, Kerouac went out alone, got drunk, hired a black prostitute for the evening, and called Cassady to urge him to come out and join in the fun. Cassady, lying to Carolyn, said he had to go spring Kerouac from jail, and the next morning, the two men arrived at the house with their hooker in tow. Carolyn, furious, threw them all out, and the two men didn't return until that evening. (Meanwhile, only a week later, in New York City, Kerouac's wife Joan gave birth to a girl she named Janet Michelle Kerouac, an event that would haunt Kerouac and intermittently complicate his life.) And although this speed bump in the Cassady house was eventually smoothed over, and all appeared to be forgiven, things got weirder when Cassady, leaving to work in San Luis Obispo for a couple of weeks, subtly suggested that Carolyn and Kerouac should have an affair while he was gone. Insulted, Carolyn did nothing, scolding Neal when he returned, but Cassady insisted that he truly would be fine with sharing her with Kerouac. Still hurt, and doubting the veracity of such statements, Carolyn ultimately decided to test Cassady.

One night, after he left for work and the children had gone to bed, she allegedly seduced Kerouac. Thus began their on-again, off-again affair, and although it was begun under Cassady's encouragement, Kerouac and Carolyn were nonetheless discreet about their lovemaking—doing it only when Cassady was away—and the relationship between the three became, curiously, more tightly-knit than ever. Suddenly, for example, the men asked Carolyn to come along with them for a night out instead of leaving her with the kids, and Cassady spent more time at home. Jack and Neal also began taping their conversations during this time, including recorded contributions from random strangers they sometimes brought home specifically for this purpose. (Many times, Jack and Neal were high during these marathon talk sessions, and very few taped fragments from this time remain; according to Carolyn, the family was so poor that they had to keep re-using the same reel-to-reel tapes again and again, thus repeatedly erasing over past conversations. Nonetheless, Jack transcribed a number of them, and they appear, in fragments, in *Visions of Cody*.) Though everyone seemed content with the living arrangement, in April, the Cassadys headed to Nashville to see Carolyn's family; they dropped off Kerouac along the way in New Mexico to catch a bus.

He intended to go to Mexico City, where Burroughs lived, and where feeding one's vices was significantly cheaper than in America. Kerouac made his way to his old friend, and the two enjoyed each other's company for a time, abusing morphine and marijuana. Burroughs, still shocked and grieving for Joan, felt cheered by his old friend's presence and took Kerouac hiking, in the mountains, and target shooting. Kerouac's thoughts turned to his childhood then, after Cassady had urged him to broaden the span of his reflection. To this end, Kerouac contemplated his early years and began writing his Bildungsroman, *Dr. Sax*.

Most of the novel was composed while Kerouac smoked pot in Burroughs' Mexico City bathroom. (He smoked there not only to escape the regular stream of partying guests, but also because given Burroughs' troubles with the law, Bill was paranoid about the smell lingering in the apartment if police came by.) In part, the physical figure of Dr. Sax was modeled on Burroughs, though Kerouac, at the time of its composition, kept this from his friend. The hallucinogenic-fueled book became Kerouac's own personal favorite of all his works, blending together the dark imaginings of childhood with an adult's sense of universal order. But back in the real world, tension arose between Kerouac and Burroughs, both because Burroughs had begun sexually courting Jack (cutting off his food supply as blackmail) and because of money. Burroughs grew tired of Kerouac's constant free-loading, and by the end of June, Kerouac—having begged for twenty dollars from Burroughs—headed to North Carolina to reach the home of his sister, Nin, and Gabrielle, who was basically working as Nin and Paul's housekeeper to earn her keep.

Meanwhile, in New York, Ginsberg worked at an advertising agency and tried to act as an agent for both Kerouac and Burroughs, eventually landing the work of both at Ace Books (a brand primarily associated with hard-boiled mysteries and pulp romances). Carl Solomon, a publisher at Ace who befriended Ginsberg while he was being evaluated in a psychiatric hospital (and the man to whom "Howl" is dedicated), got frustrated with Kerouac's constant stalling, however, and in retaliation, sent a letter of encouragement to Neal; in it, Solomon told Neal that he was a better storyteller than Kerouac and, therefore, Neal shouldn't listen to him; needless to say, this infuriated Kerouac, and the news from the East wasn't getting better any time soon. In July, when Kerouac returned to New York, the editors at Ace wanted Kerouac to cut sections from his novel, which wrankled him, as did the fact that Joan Haverty Kerouac had called Harcourt Brace in order to track down her child's deadbeat dad.

To avoid any run-ins with the law, Kerouac hightailed it back across the country, hitchhiking out to Neal and Carolyn's new home in San Jose. Neal got Kerouac a job as a brakeman, and although Jack hated it, he valued and enjoyed the exposure the job provided him to vagrants and hobos (always a point of fascination to him), many of whom he'd observe at the end of the line. At home, Kerouac resumed his affair with Carolyn, and despite Cassady's previous insistence about "being fine" with such a situation, jealousy inevitably began to create small ruptures in the men's friendship; indeed, the house soon became too small for their attention-hungry egos, and finally, one night, after the two men argued over a pork chop, Kerouac packed his bag and requested that Carolyn drive him to a nearby flea-bag hotel, the type that catered to the way-below-the-poverty-line community that obsessed Kerouac. (During this time, Kerouac wrote his acclaimed essay, "October in the Railroad Earth," which contains his observations from working the rails.) Seemingly, this separation between Jack and Cassady was just what they needed, for after spending some time apart, the two men reconciled and headed down to Mexico City together.

After procuring a sizable amount of marijuana, however, Cassady turned around to head back to Carolyn in California, leaving Kerouac to find Burroughs on his own. Burroughs was awaiting trial for Joan's murder, however, and soon fled the country, heading to Panama by way of Florida. Alone again, Kerouac rented an adobe hut on the roof of a building for twelve dollars a month and befriended an ex-Times Square coat thief junkie (and friend of Burroughs) named Bill Garver. While Kerouac, with Garver's help, slipped back into his benzadrine addiction, he was still lonely, urging Holmes, Ginsberg, and Carolyn Cassady to come to Mexico City.

No one took Kerouac up on the offer, though. While he used the opportunity to get some writing done, he soon decided that instead of spending Christmas 1952 alone in Mexico, he wanted to travel to Gabrielle's home in Richmond Hill, Queens. Once there, he watched television, drank beer, and spent three months writing the complete manuscript for what would become *Maggie Cassidy*, a novel about his high school love, Mary Carney. The novel's focus, of course, indicates that Kerouac was not just reflecting, but seriously pondering, his relationships with women at this time, presumably due to his confusion about Carolyn. In many ways, though, Mary Carney would remain, throughout Kerouac's life, his romantic ideal—though the reality had clearly been more complicated than his tightly-held, rose-colored memory—and he would spend years questioning whether he'd missed his big opportunity at happiness by refusing to settle with her in Lowell after high school.

In addition to Kerouac's personal ennui, multiple reasons for frustration regarding his professional writing life stacked up during this time: Burroughs' book, *Junky*, was about to be released by Ace; Holmes' Beat novel *Go!* had received much attention; and rejections for *On the Road* continued to pile up. Although Malcolm Cowley at Viking provided Kerouac a reason to be optimistic, saying that he would recommend the novel for publication, Kerouac was by this time so jaded that he refused to invest his hopes anymore. Moving first to Montreal, intending to work for Canadian Pacific Railroad, Kerouac soon decided it was too cold and lonely in Canada and headed back out to California. Frustrated in his efforts to re-ignite his affair with Carolyn (Neal was home with an ankle injury), Kerouac resumed his job as a brakeman for a short time.

Kerouac then got what would be his last opportunity to work on board a ship, this time heading for war-torn Korea. True to pattern, however, Kerouac got fired from his job as an officers' saloon waiter when he failed to show up for his shift while the *S.S. William Carruth* was docked in Mobile, Alabama. Thus relieved from duties, Kerouac headed back to Gabrielle in Richmond Hill (though he did get an essay, "Slobs of the Kitchen Sea," from the experience, which he later included in *Lonesome Traveler*). And although he felt good about the writing he was doing, he learned, upon his return, that Holmes had received a $20,000 advance for his novel about the Beats, *Go*, as well as positive reviews and related assignments from the *New York Times*, which did little to lift Kerouac's spirits.

On one of his many trips into Manhattan to visit his friends, however, Kerouac met a small-bodied, beautiful, black woman named Alene Lee, and while she initially had reservations about Jack, he was drawn to her immediately. (Her name was kept secret for many years; though interviewed by early Kerouac biographers, she was only referred to then as Mardou Fox, the pseudonym assigned her by Kerouac in *The Subterraneans*.) Lee worked in publishing, specifically with health books, and to Kerouac, she appeared to represent all that was exotic and hip while broadcasting an intense sexuality. Previously, she had befriended and spent time with junkies, causing her family to send her to a psychiatric hospital; when she was released, she went right back into the arms of that crowd, drifting around the Village, going to parties, smoking pot, and staying with whomever would take her in. After one party at Ginsberg's, which had become a Village hangout for those interested in jazz, poetry, and drugs, Alene and Kerouac became close; but there were soon problems.

Alene, who now reportedly says that she never took Kerouac seriously as a lover, once told him that he was too old to live with his mother, which incensed him. In turn, she was enraged when she discovered that Kerouac lied about her ethnicity, telling Lucien Carr that she was half Indian, not half African American; and one night, he chose to spend the night with famed essayist Gore Vidal rather than her, causing her to stomp off, fuming, into the New York night (an event alluded to in *The Subterraneans*). After a couple of months in the eye of this stormy relationship, Kerouac locked himself away for three days and wrote *The Subterraneans*, a novella-length book about his unconventional, highly erotic affair with Alene. Judging from this account, sex appears to have been the relationship's core, since Kerouac never stayed the night, but rather hurried off in the pre-dawn hours to be at Gabrielle's before she woke and have breakfast with her. (Knowing also how this affair would disturb racist Gabrielle, Kerouac urged her never to read *The Subterraneans*.)

And while Kerouac was proud of his artistic accomplishment with this novel (and wrote "Essentials of Spontaneous Prose" at the urging of his friends afterward, a list that described his writing method and philosophy), when he took the manuscript to his girlfriend to read, Alene felt violated, horrified that her intimate, personal conversations and actions had been transcribed and exposed in order to provide, quite literally, the whole of the novel's content. She also realized, however, that Kerouac was extremely vulnerable, having received rejection after rejection for his work while his friends got published; so instead of asking him to set fire to the book—which he offered to do—she only asked that he change some details regarding the setting and her ethnic background (making her part Native American in order to better disguise her identity). But in spite of this compromise, the relationship was doomed, and in fact, it fell apart, reportedly leaving Kerouac depressed.

Another friend of Ginsberg's who entered Kerouac's life at this time was a poet named Gregory Corso, who was then only twenty-three years old. A Village native, he'd been left on his own at a young age—after the death of his mother and his father's abandonment—so he'd been in institutions and jails during most of his short life. While in prison, he'd begun to write poetry, and one night, after being released, he was sitting in a Village bar writing when Ginsberg approached him. Corso's poems impressed him, and he soon invited the young poet to be part of his artistic social circle. Thus, in the summer of 1953, Corso met Kerouac, among others; the perpetually competitive Kerouac, not surprisingly, seemed initially condescending toward Corso, presenting himself as the older, wiser, more experienced writer. Reportedly, though, Corso once went to Alene's place once to wait for Kerouac, and she forcibly seduced the poet. This upset Kerouac, but things had been deteriorating between the couple, anyway. This event only confirmed that the relationship should end.

This low point left Kerouac searching in new places for comfort and peace, a search that would result in a temporary shift in his perspective—one that might have saved him from himself, had he been able to adopt it wholeheartedly.

CHAPTER FIVE

Buddhism and the Beats

'I see a vision of a great rucksack revolution,' he wrote, 'millions of young Americans wandering around ... giving visions of eternal freedom to every-body.... How truly great and wise America will be, with all this energy and exuberance ... focused on the Dharma.

—Jack Kerouac, qtd. in *Subterranean Kerouac: The Hidden Life of Jack Kerouac*

AT THIS TIME in 1953, Kerouac sought solace in Thoreau as well as in Buddhist texts (Ginsberg had stirred Kerouac's initial interest in the latter subject). He translated sutras from French and, eventually, wrote a biography of the Buddha (posthumously published) called *Wake Up!* Although Catholicism was the spiritual thread that ran seamlessly through Kerouac's life, he felt that the church didn't soothe his anxieties regarding his failure to publish again, while Buddhism seemed to offer peace and philosophical consolation. (Some scholars argue that Kerouac merely adopted the parts of Buddhism that made his vices seem acceptable—justified by the idea that everything was an illusion and didn't matter anyway—thus enabling him to continue in his ways rather than change.) Thoreau, on the other hand, convinced him that he needed to return to nature and live simply, emphasizing complete self-reliance, something that had never been Kerouac's strong suit.

In early 1954, Kerouac moved back to San Jose to live with the Cassadys again, and he continued his study of Buddhism, keeping a notebook wherein he struggled to translate texts for Ginsberg. These notes soon sprawled out, however, into a huge, explorative personal study, veering off frequently into Kerouac's thoughts and observations, prayers, meditations, and poems; in this way, the notebook became a tangible display of one Westerner's struggle to grapple with eastern thought (the notebooks would later be published, posthumously, as *Some of the Dharma*). The main tenets of Buddhism that Kerouac tried to embrace was the idea that everything was a kind of dream or illusion except the mind, which was part of the Universal Mind Essence—a slight variation on Emerson's Oversoul, or God—and that acceptance of this idea would eliminate all anxieties one normally has, including the fear of death, a strong holdover from Kerouac's childhood trauma with Gerard. This also, of course, lended itself to his favored style of writing; indeed, Buddhism, in a way, seemed to sanction, ideologically, Kerouac's no-revision, spontaneous prose as being the pure essence of his consciousness: "Technique in writing, for Kerouac, was not 'changing words and halting and erasing and rearranging,' but finding 'deep form, as ored up from the bottom of the Mind unplanned' ... *the secret of writing is in the rhythm of urgency*" (Amburn, 197).

Neal Cassady, as well as Carolyn, had begun a different kind of spiritual journey, though; instead of Buddhism, Cassady felt drawn to Edgar Cayce and his theories regarding reincarnation. He and Kerouac argued and discussed their respective causes for hours on end. Like Burroughs, however, Cassady reached a point at which he grew frustrated with Kerouac's free-loading, and after an argument over how to split up a bag of marijuana, Kerouac holed up in a cheap hotel temporarily, then bolted for the East Coast again to live with Gabrielle in Richmond Hill. Once there, he continued to work on a collection of poetry, *San Francisco Blues*, which he had begun in California while at the Cameo, his semi-regular flophouse, and *Book of Dreams*, in which Kerouac reported the story of his dreams in spontaneous prose. Battling alcoholism, Kerouac began to experiment with putting a stop to his drinking (as well as his sexual habits) for a time, wanting to live in the way of Buddhism; unfortunately, though, he couldn't stay on the wagon for long, and his guilt over his inability to be disciplined left him feeling more ashamed than ever.

For once, though, instead of striking out for the west coast, Kerouac bought a bus ticket to Lowell, thinking that his hometown might provide him with solace. He visited his old haunts, including his boyhood church, where he re-considered the spiritual dimension of the "beat" concept; when he returned home, he resumed his Buddhist studies with newfound zeal, now more convinced than ever that spirituality was where the answers, for him, would lie. He considered Cassady's belief in reincarnation more seriously, thinking that Cassady might in fact be Gerard re-born, but these new ideas and thoughts greatly troubled Gabrielle, who saw her son veering dangerously far away from Catholicism. Also, during this time, Joan Haverty summoned Kerouac back into court regarding child support; this infuriated Gabrielle all the more, since she was still having to support her grown son. *Some of the Dharma,* at this point, included Kerouac's thoughts and observations while confronting these two exasperated women (Joan and Gabrielle) in his life.

When Kerouac came into court to face Joan, in January 1955, he denied paternity yet again. But he also saw Joan's daughter, Jan, for the first time, and in a letter to Ginsberg, Kerouac admitted to the striking resemblance she bore to him. Paternity was of no matter in the end, though; Kerouac was able to produce a doctor's note regarding his phlebitis, stating that he couldn't sustain full-time employment because of health reasons. The matter was suspended for one year, and Joan Haverty didn't press the matter. Kerouac, prepared for the worst, came to trial prepared to go to prison, carrying a manilla folder with hundreds of pages of notes and the Buddhist bible. Interestingly, after the ruling, he made a point of showing these materials to Joan and telling her about his newest project, though she dismissed the whole enterprise as a silly flight of fancy. Ultimately, she told Kerouac that if he didn't try to see their daughter (there seemed little danger of that), she wouldn't demand child support, and the two parted again, Kerouac more determined than ever to make Buddhism a way of life rather than a mere interest.

In the spring, he moved with the recently-retired Gabrielle to Nin's house in Rocky Mount, and while he continued to study, translate, write, and meditate, his sister and her husband grew impatient, wondering when exactly he was going to get a job or leave their home. Watching Kerouac sit in the yard in a lawn chair, drinking what he called "moonshine cocktails" (orange juice, ginger ale, and white lightning), Nin grew more and more bitter; she was already angry about, and suspicious of, his Buddhist pursuits, but watching Jack sit for hours, while everyone around him worked, fueled the flame that much more.

Feeling under fire, Jack borrowed ten dollars from Gabrielle and hitchhiked back to New York. He met with editors and agents there, but none of them seemed able to do much toward getting *Dr. Sax* or *The Subterraneans* published. He slept on the floor of friends' apartments as long as his money lasted, then headed back to Rocky Mount. Elsewhere in the world—in Tangier, Morocco, to be specific—Burroughs, who had never supported Kerouac's interest in Buddhism, received letters from Kerouac that detailed his work on a science fiction story called "cityCityCITY," wherein steel plate covered the overpopulated earth and computers controlled the world. Fellow Buddhist Ginsberg, meanwhile, got "recommended reading" lists and translated sutras. But given the tension regarding both finances and religion at Nin's house, Kerouac knew he couldn't stay there much longer.

Soon, Kerouac headed back to Mexico City by himself, hoping to forget the string of rejections that he'd received for his works at various publishing houses, despite the Malcolm Cowley-sponsored April publication of an *On the Road* excerpt in *New World Writing* and the upcoming publication of his chapter about Bea, "The Mexican Girl," in the *Paris Review*. (Kerouac hadn't wanted to break up his novel into digestible pieces, but Cowley convinced him that it would work toward publication of the novel, of which Kerouac was, by then, already tiring. Significantly, though,

Kerouac angered Cowley when he published under the pseudonym "Jean-Louis," which he did to avoid being sued again by
Joan for child support.) Once Kerouac was south of the border, he
hoped to live simply and embrace the tenets of Buddhist living; to
this end, he rented a damp, smelly, rustic room, with no electricity,
on the roof of a house. With only candles and a brakeman's
lantern for lighting, he daily made his way up flights of stairs, past
the sound of families and music, to the building's top, where he
kept his clothes, Christian and Buddhist bibles, notebooks, paper,
airmail envelopes, and copies of each of his novel manuscripts. He
appeared to eschew the company of prostitutes for a while, though
he still availed himself freely of Mexico City's abundant supply of
cheap booze and drugs. His main source for the latter, was a prostitute named Esperanza Villanueva, the heroin-addicted, young,
Catholic widow of Burroughs' former dealer.

Unlike the intellectual women in Manhattan, Esperanza
seemed, in Kerouac's mind, to live truthfully and naturally in the
spirit of Buddhism, though she knew nothing of its tenets. Kerouac fell in love with her instantly, it seems, finding her sadness
irresistible and familiar; their affair inspired the novel, *Tristessa*. In
this book, Kerouac's Madonna/whore complex regarding women
culminates clearly in the figure of the title character, who, despite
selling sex, seems to possess a patience, resignation, and nobility
aligned with the Virgin Mary. At this time, Kerouac also hung out
with Burroughs' old friend, William Garver—now a sixty-year-old
man who lived on a trust fund—and worked on the poems that
would compose *Mexico City Blues*; often, these poems stemmed
from his conversations with Garver, with whom Kerouac spent
much of his time getting stoned. Kerouac viewed Garver as a his-
torian and scholar rather than a deadbeat, and this is how he
stumbled upon the idea of keeping careful notes of their exchanges
and turning them into poems.

Kerouac's emotional state during this time is a point of contention among biographers: Nicosia outright rejects the idea of
Kerouac having a relationship with Esperanza; Amburn claims he
was wholly content with the affair and thus very productive,
writing some of his best work; Charters believes Kerouac could

not get past his racism enough to have a relationship with Esperanza; and Gifford and Lee believe he stuck to the course of abstinence, taking his new Buddhist beliefs and philosophies to heart. While we can never know for certain who is right, we can rely, to some degree, on the accuracy with which Kerouac kept his records. Though he took liberties with the truth when writing his autobiographical novels, he seems to have been assiduous in maintaining his personal correspondence and archives, feeling sure all along that he would be the literary star he was in fact destined to be.

Back in California, Ginsberg was contending with the direction of his life—deciding to enroll in UC Berkeley's master's program in English—and with the poem "Howl" in its nascent stages. But the year leading up to Kerouac's return in September 1955 saw Ginsberg struggling to define himself. The poet had originally headed out west to live with the Cassadys, assuring Carolyn that his erotic fixation with Cassady had long since passed. However, when she came home one day and found Ginsberg and Cassady engaged in sexual activity, she threw Ginsberg out, an exodus that led him to venture out and meet up with the artistic crowd of San Francisco's North Beach. Members of this community included poet Michael McClure, poet/publisher Lawrence Ferlinghetti, and Kenneth Rexroth, who hosted poetry readings in his house. Ginsberg found himself newly at home among these political radicals, but he was still reticent about his sexuality. And despite his best efforts to "go straight"—he acquired a girlfriend, got a job doing market research, and sought out psychiatrists for guidance—he eventually gave up such appearances when one psychiatrist finally encouraged him to live by his natural urges and desires for men rather than repress them. Soon, by way of his acquaintance with the artist Robert LaVigne, Ginsberg met a young man who had once modeled for a painting: Peter Orlovsky. Shortly thereafter, the two men moved in together, beginning a serious, long term relationship, and Ginsberg, utterly in love, began work on his masterpiece, "Howl."

Thus, when Kerouac returned to California, Ginsberg, tinkering still with his poem, was in the midst of planning a poetry reading at new avant-garde gallery called the Six Gallery, in San Francisco. Though invited to participate, Kerouac was too shy. Instead, the spotlight-phobic Kerouac collected money for wine and sat at the stage's edge as Ginsberg—as well as Rexroth, McClure, Philip Whalen, Gary Snyder, and Philip Lamantia—read from their work. During the reading, Kerouac passed jugs of cheap wine down the rows of listeners to share, and he occasionally yelled "Go!" to the poets, as he might to a jazz musician, mid-solo. "Howl" instantly registered with the audience, and the one hundred and fifty people in that room who heard it first knew they had witnessed something groundbreaking. With its jazz-inspired spontaneity, graphic imagery, and gritty, vernacular lexicon, "Howl" seemed destined to send American poetry into bohemian clubs and coffee houses.

And although Kerouac himself was not formally a part of this event, the reading proved to be an important turning point for him nonetheless. While Ginsberg lost himself in "Howl"'s success, partying, getting high, and undressing in public, Kerouac sat on the margins at these parties, drinking but also noting other people's conversations. He was shy, of course, but his isolation was more than this; it fed off of his anxiety about being an outsider. And even though he made excuses, citing the fact that the poets were too intellectual and removed from the real world for him to relate to them, the reality was that insecurity was taking over his sense of himself; his middle-class aspirations, along with his confidence in being a successful, published writer was thrown in doubt.

But fortunately at this time, Kerouac finally found two practicing fellow Buddhists—the poets Philip Whalen and Gary Snyder—to whom he could talk extensively. Upon spending more time with Snyder, verbally sparring, arguing against the intellectualism of Zen Buddhism, Kerouac received an invitation to climb a peak with him (and a librarian named John Montgomery) in the Sierra Nevada. Anxious to learn how to be a Buddhist hermit who could live off the land without the comforts of civilization (Kerouac's daydream at this time), Kerouac accepted the offer, knowing Snyder could teach him much in regard to survival skills. Montgomery and Snyder were experienced climbers and hiked to the peak with ease (Snyder characteristically going part of the way naked), but Kerouac struggled, as noted in the novel he wrote about the experience, *The Dharma Bums*. As Amburn explained,

> Kerouac's account of the climb in *The Dharma Bums* is a spectacular foray into nature writing and bull's-eye prophecy. A vision comes to him on the mountaintop, revealing that his mission is to lead humanity and incite a generation of young people to drop out of the rat race and hit the road. (231)

Additionally, the novel bore witness to the battle raging in Kerouac regarding his spiritual beliefs; his Catholic family scoffed at his Buddhist interests and research, worried that his soul was in danger, and no matter how much he wished to adopt the Buddhist tenets as completely as Snyder had, Kerouac seemed incapable of ever freeing himself from the grip of Catholicism.

Another event included in *The Dharma Bums* involved Neal Cassady, whose newly acquired mistress, Natalie Jackson, had attended the Six Gallery reading with him. Separated from her husband, and mother to a child who was then in her parents' custody, Natalie appears to have been an emotionally vulnerable and fragile young woman; though she and Cassady seemed happy and in love at the Six Gallery, Kerouac found her in a very different state upon his return from hiking with Snyder and Montgomery. In the interim, Cassady had reportedly coerced her into forging Carolyn's signature on a check, which provided him money for gambling at the track (all of which, of course, he promptly lost). This unsuccessful scheme sent Natalie over the edge, and from her gaunt appearance and haunted expression, Kerouac got the impression that she was in the eye of a nervous breakdown. Cassady, frantic and needing to leave her apartment to go to work, begged Kerouac to stay with her, afraid of what she would do to herself if left alone.

Paranoid with guilt, Natalie envisioned that she and Cassady would be arrested, and he'd already stopped her once from cutting her wrists. Kerouac reluctantly agreed to stay with her, and after Cassady left, he tried to get Natalie to eat something. Shaking, she refused, and the two began yelling nonsense to each other. Natalie babbled urgently about the seriousness of her claims, and Kerouac, in response, became angry and vehemently insisted that she should adopt more Buddhist perspectives. It struck him then that she, along with everyone else, wasn't truly listening to what he had to say on the topic, and this frustrated him. Fortunately, though, after the two stayed on this conversational merry-go-round for a good while, Cassady returned. But all these efforts came to naught; in the pre-dawn glow of the next day, Natalie jumped from her building's roof. This tragedy shook Kerouac to his core, and he grew restless to move again, setting his sights this time on his sister's home in North Carolina. He wanted to spend Christmas with his family again.

To this end, he hitchhiked and rode busses his way east in December, 1955, and once there, while trying to recover from what the California newspapers had dubbed a "bohemian suicide," Kerouac worked again to marry the beliefs of Catholicism and Buddhism in his mind. The artistic result of this exploration is the novel *Visions of Gerard*, a work wherein Kerouac tries to reconcile himself, finally, to the childhood death of his supposedly saintly brother, using the frameworks of both Buddhist and Catholic beliefs. Nin and Gabrielle still railed against these Eastern influences on Jack, but he was feeling better than he had in some time, performing yoga headstands for five minutes each morning to cure the pain, from the thrombophlebitis, in his legs; the practice, which he picked up from a bum in Los Angeles the year before, appeared to work, and Kerouac continued this ritual for much of his life. However, despite his temporary happiness in Rocky Mount, writing, revising, and meditating, Kerouac only stayed until spring, when he planned to head out west again to pursue a new, temporary job. Inspired by Philip Whalen, who had previously worked in this capacity, and yearning for isolation from the world, Kerouac had applied for a job as a fire-warden in Washington. He did, in fact, receive a post, which would last for two months; he was scheduled to start training in June, 1956.

In anticipation of this, Kerouac returned to Snyder's rustic, bare bones cabin in California in April, where he worked on two new projects: the spontaneous prose experiment *Old Angel Midnight*, and a Buddhist sutra called *The Scripture of the Golden Eternity*. On March 18, 1956, a repeat performance of the Six Gallery reading was scheduled in a makeshift theater in Berkeley, and while a pre-reading spaghetti dinner at Ginsberg's was tense and uncomfortable—Orlovsky and Ginsberg were living apart and trying to date women again—the reading was, once again, electrifying. It must be noted, of course, that this San Francisco poetry culture flourished, in part, by way of the famous paperback bookstore called City Lights. As a new venture, Lawrence Ferlinghetti, the store's co-founder, had just recently begun publishing the "Pocket Poets Series," which produced small, inexpensive, paperback collections, thus making poetry more accessible to everyone. (Indeed, "Howl" was in its last editing stages that spring, after Ginsberg rejected an offer to publish it in an expensive limited edition.)

Snyder left for two years in Japan on May 15th, and Kerouac was left to his own devices in his friend's small cabin. Kerouac was likely relieved at being alone temporarily—Snyder had begun to criticize Kerouac's drinking and laziness—but was probably also worse off. In some ways, he went further into his shell, hiding in the dim corners of his friends' parties while throwing back large quantities of wine. (His friends guessed that this was simply his shyness kicking in, but larger insecurities likely played a role as well.) Another poet, Robert Creeley, eventually moved into Snyder's cabin (called Marin-An) with Kerouac, and the two men got along well. But when the time arrived, Kerouac hitchhiked his way up the West Coast to attend his ranger training and assume his position on Desolation Peak.

In a moment of optimism, Kerouac had fantasized that this post, removing him as it would from the seductive, worldly vices of drugs, alcohol, and women, would allow him the opportunity to meditate and write; naively, he believed that these things would be enough, and that he would be content. Instead, what he experienced during the two months at his post was blinding boredom—which drove him to play the fantasy baseball game he'd played with cards as a child—accompanied by neuroses regarding his lifetime of mistakes and poor decisions. In this way, a precedent was set for Kerouac; again and again, he would come back to this ideal, thinking that he would be happy and productive in isolation from the world, when the truth was that during these times, he ultimately became utterly, inconsolably miserable. At war, clearly, were the ways in which Kerouac wished to see himself versus who he actually was.

But while he holed up in his post, an undercurrent of interest in the Beats was about to break in the American press. The *New York Times*, *Mademoiselle*, and *Life* magazine were all preparing stories related to the Beat writers, and "Howl" was on the brink of publication. With this momentum behind the Beats, Viking finally agreed to publish *On the Road*. After coming down from Desolation Peak, though, Kerouac concerned himself with more earthly desires, viewing multiple burlesque shows in Seattle, and then made his way down to San Francisco. In seeming celebration of their first tastes of fame, Kerouac and many of his friends made their way to Mexico, once again. While Kerouac remained disciplined at first, refusing drugs and sex and working diligently on *Tristessa* and *Old Angel Midnight*, his self-control soon faltered.

After two months in Mexico, the partying band of artists returned to New York on the verge of stardom. Though *On the Road* wouldn't be published until 1957, the following year, Kerouac's phone was already ringing. Reporters and writers from magazines around the world wanted his thoughts and opinions, since he had already been deemed the avatar of cool. It seemed as though Kerouac finally had his foot in the world's door and would gain the recognition and fame that had eluded him for so long.

CHAPTER SIX

Fame

*From a letter, discussing a visit to the apartment of
some of Kerouac's 'disciples': "They think they're
doing what I'd want them to do. They're fucking in
front of me, but all I can see is thighs."*
—quoted in *Kerouac: A Biography*

BEFORE *ON THE ROAD* COULD be published, Kerouac had to
spend hours on end with the man who had tirelessly championed
the book, editor Malcolm Cowley, to make painstaking revisions
to avoid potential legal problems (regarding the use of living per-
sons' words, actions, etc.). And while Kerouac had waited for this
opportunity for years, he nonetheless grew petulant and depressed
at this time. His drinking spiked, and in February, 1957, he made
arrangements to visit Burroughs in Morocco—specifically, the
port of Tangier, where Burroughs had lived for the past two years.
As in Mexico City, Tangier was reported to offer an endless supply
of sex and booze and drugs at next-to-nothing prices; after Kerouac's arrival, though, he quickly became disenchanted.

Before continuing on his way to explore Europe, earlier than
originally planned, Kerouac helped Burroughs with the novel he
helped name *Naked Lunch*, typing it and offering suggestions. In
March, Ginsberg arrived in Tangier with his lover, Peter Orlovsky,

and announced that "Howl" had spawned an obscenity trial that was scheduled for June in San Francisco. This pleased Ginsberg to no end; having worked in the field of advertising, he knew well that not only would the surrounding controversy boost sales of the poem enormously, but that the attention would also catapult him into the spotlight as Beat spokesman. Once, when his efforts to invite celebrities to a reading failed—out of Marlon Brando, Aldous Huxley, and Anais Nin, only Nin showed—Ginsberg committed an act of desperation in order to get the media's attention: he stripped naked, claiming that "The poet always stands naked before the world!" Nothing could more clearly demonstrate the differences between Kerouac and Ginsberg; while Ginsberg was a social, public animal who saw the larger picture and manipulated the media for his own political and artistic purposes, Kerouac felt jittery about being photographed and interviewed, shying away from many such opportunities. Though often closely associated in the public's mind, the two men were, in many ways, diametrically opposed. In Tangier, Ginsberg held court among the Beats, but Kerouac already found himself disenchanted with the group and the lifestyle, once remarking: "To think that I had so much to do with it, too, in fact at that very moment the manuscript of *Road* was being linotyped for imminent publication and I was already sick of the whole subject" (Amburn, 267).

In April, Kerouac made his way from Morocco to France, where he did some sightseeing before going on to London and then home to New York. Considering a move out to California, he and Gabrielle briefly rented an apartment in Berkeley. He eventually moved his mother back down to Florida and fled yet again to Mexico City, hoping to concentrate on his writing for a few weeks.

Upon his return to New York, *On the Road* was on the verge of publication. He began an affair then with a twenty-one year old woman named Joyce Glassman, a writer who was with Kerouac when, before dawn on September 5, they went to buy one of the day's first copies of the *New York Times*. Flipping the pages to find the review, Kerouac was finally rewarded: critic Gilbert Millstein not only praised *On the Road*, but hailed it as important and masterful. Kerouac reportedly seemed more puzzled than happy in response, perhaps in shock, but perhaps also confused by the huge gap that existed between Millstein's accolades and what Kerouac had heard from publishers for years. And clearly, there was some wisdom to be found in Kerouac's cautious reserve; for while Millstein indeed lauded Kerouac's achievement, reviewers for other publications—some of which were traditionally conservative—were not so kind, criticizing the writing as poor, the content as deliberately sensational without substance, and the plot as frustratingly tangential and non-linear. But such criticisms may have only intensified the curiosity of the public—a stifled public that seemed hungry, on some level, for something raw, unconventional, and honest. Elvis Presley had scandalously shaken his hips on *The Ed Sullivan Show* only months before; now Kerouac was shaking perspectives.

Not surprisingly, though, the media made a reductive caricature of Kerouac well before he had a chance to get his bearings; magazine reporters called upon him endlessly to explain to them—so they could report to their readers—what phrases, clothes, habits, etc. were cool and hip, and which were not (a convention still in use in today's magazines). He was suddenly on the guest list of every party, and suddenly, too, all those manuscripts that had sat in idle stacks for so long were in demand. Grove Press contacted Kerouac's agent, promising to publish *The Subterraneans* as is, with no revisions, and Viking called, wanting to discuss his next project. Kerouac saw this quick thrust into fame as an opportunity, so he sat down to write—in a manic, Benzadrine-driven two week period—*The Dharma Bums*, a book about hiking the Sierra Nevada with Gary Snyder and John Montgomery.

Kerouac got pulled far out from this frenzy, however, when a Manhattan club called the Village Vanguard contacted him and asked if he would be willing, for one week, to perform on their stage in conjunction with jazz performers. Still insecure about his work—despite years of arrogant blustering—Kerouac nonetheless read poems from *Mexico City Blues*, interspersed between those written by Ginsberg and Corso. Although the quality of these evening performances varied—Kerouac was normally drunk, seeking liquid courage to overcome his nerves—he was accompanied one night by the television star Steve Allen, an accomplished jazz pianist in his own right, and the collaboration was a huge success. As a result, Kerouac and Allen were approached to record an album together, which they did; the album was well received by critics as well as popular audiences.

Otherwise, though, the critical assault on Kerouac's written work never ceased, particularly as more and more of it made its way out into the public sphere over a short period of time. *The Subterraneans* was panned by reviewers, one of whom not only remarked that Kerouac's work showed a lack of imagination, but also that Kerouac championed incoherence and ignorance. San Francisco poet Kenneth Rexroth, venomously doling out payback—Kerouac had known about Rexroth's wife having an affair with Robert Creeley in San Francisco and didn't tell Rexroth about it, a choice for which Rexroth punished him in print throughout Kerouac's life—publicly humiliated Kerouac at every opportunity through his reviews. What most bothered Kerouac, though, was the repeated association that critics made between his work and the iconic teen rebel figures that currently filled movie screens. Movies like Marlon Brando's *The Wild Ones* and James Dean's *Rebel Without a Cause* repelled Kerouac, who abhorred their depiction of seemingly unjustified, superfluous violence. To him, the connection just didn't make sense; the greasy-haired, lazy, mumbling members of this new youth movement seemed to have little to nothing in common with the manic excitement he and Cassady and Ginsberg had felt in their youth, burning to go everywhere, and to see and to learn and to experience everything. (To Kerouac's chagrin, the film made later that same year, based on Kerouac's book, *The Subterraneans*, did nothing to dispel these cartoonish notions of the Beats, but rather only reinforced them.)

Depressed by this turn of events—as well as by everyone now knowing about his worst addictions and actions through his confessional writing—and feeling out of control of his own image and life's work, Kerouac holed up with his mother in a new Northport, Long Island home, where he drank heavily while assuming, ironically, the bourgeois suburban habits of watching television and gardening. Tired already of the limelight, he adjusted to this quiet, reclusive life, and for perhaps the first time in his life, he was financially comfortable, having banked the money for film rights (Tri-Way Films had bought *On the Road*) as well as for the works that had previously floated around publishing offices without response. Gabrielle managed all the money, though; she and Jack shared an account—so her signature had to accompany his on any check he wrote—and she allowed Jack only so much for beer and cigarettes. The royalties from *On the Road* were largely invested in the house's mortgage, such that Gabrielle insisted they didn't have enough money to install a phone, and Kerouac was left to walk a mile to a pay phone in order to contact his friends in New York.

One journalist, Alfred Aronowitz, came to the house to interview Kerouac, and through his *New York Post* articles, the public learned about the state of Kerouac's personal life: he normally slept until noon, then got up and started drinking immediately while writing for a while before "breakfast." During this period of his life, however, Kerouac was soon shaken up by the news, delivered via a letter from Carolyn, that Neal Cassady had been arrested on the Fourth of July for selling two joints to undercover narcotics officers. This offense, teamed with Cassady's auto-theft-riddled juvenile record, landed him in San Quentin, where he whiled away the time exploring the tenets of his original religion: Catholicism.

Kerouac, meanwhile, isolated himself to work on both *Book of Dreams* and a collection of travel essays called *Lonesome Traveler*. There would be no break in the monotony of his daily life for a while, since Gabrielle had written insulting letters to Burroughs and Ginsberg, warning them both to stay away from her son and to stop corrupting him. Kerouac himself did absolutely nothing to defend his friends or go against his mother's wishes (despite the fact that Ginsberg nearly always remained loyal and defended his friend vociferously, no matter what the circumstances, to the end). Eventually, however, in early 1959, Kerouac and photographer Robert Frank hatched an idea for an experimental film, *Pull My Daisy*, which would be drawn from one act of a play Kerouac wrote in 1957. The movie's plot involves a progressive bishop visiting the Cassadys in their California home, and while Kerouac narrated the film, Ginsberg and Corso were two of the stars, thus providing a chance for Ginsberg and Kerouac to reconcile without the meddling, judgmental presence of Gabrielle.

After the film wrapped, Kerouac traveled to California to attend its premiere in San Francisco as well as to be a guest on Steve Allen's prime time show. While on television, though visibly nervous during the interview, Kerouac hit his stride once he began to read from his work while Allen played jazz piano in the background. (Characteristically, Kerouac later got drunk and confronted Allen that same night, forever ending their relationship.) And while one would expect him to visit Carolyn, and perhaps Cassady in prison, Kerouac failed to do either. Indeed, Kerouac had even made arrangements to come talk to the prisoners—as Ginsberg had also done for Neal—but then didn't show up, not bothering to call or write anyone about his change of heart. Instead, Kerouac sheepishly performed one of his typical pub crawls before making arrangements to head back to the East Coast. According to Sandison, Carolyn Cassady viewed this irresponsible, hurtful rejection by Kerouac more compassionately than would a more objective party; Kerouac later told Carolyn that he had ignored her during this time because he couldn't stand for her to see him in his current state.

So instead of confronting the Cassadys, Kerouac moved on, getting together with Philip Whalen, Lew Welch, and Albert Saijo in San Francisco. The latter two men had offered Kerouac a ride back to New York, and along the way, they composed collaborative haiku that would later be published as *Trip Trap: Haiku on the Road*. When he returned to Northport, he was left alone with Gabrielle again, and his alcoholism grew more intense. The myriad of books he had mostly written during the highly productive years between the original three-week composition and the publication of *On the Road* suddenly came off the presses in rapid succession. In 1959, *Dr. Sax* and *Maggie Cassidy* both took a brutal beating from most critics (which the thin-skinned Kerouac took personally), and in 1960, Kerouac published *Lonesome Traveler, Tristessa, Visions of Cody,* and *Scripture of the Golden Eternity*. As Kerouac's star fell, and critics and friends considered the possibility that he might be creatively empty, the man grew bloated from alcohol and was perpetually irritable and angry, seeming to have absolutely no control over himself physically or mentally.

But in the midst of this extended nadir, Lawrence Ferlinghetti made Kerouac an offer that would give the writer a chance to pull himself together. Ferlinghetti, co-owner of the legendary San Francisco bookstore and publisher City Lights, was about to go to print with Kerouac's *Book of Dreams*, and he offered Kerouac the use of a secluded cabin on the Pacific Coast to perform final revisions on this work. As Kerouac had done when he sought out a job as a fire marshal in Washington a few years before, he envisioned that he would finally be happy in the isolation of such a scaled-down, natural setting—and that he could let go of his worldly vices and get to work there—so he accepted the offer. But Kerouac made one condition: he demanded that Ferlinghetti keep his presence a secret. Ferlinghetti agreed, and Kerouac boarded a train bound for the west coast.

Despite his careful warnings to Ferlinghetti, though—and his use of aliases on correspondence related to the trip—Kerouac made a bee-line to a popular North Beach Beat hangout upon arriving in California. He spent the next few days drinking in different bars in the area, alerting everyone to his presence, and then he finally traveled to Bixby Canyon to get started on his work. Arriving at night, Kerouac made his way cautiously, stumbling through the darkness. He eventually found the cabin that would be his temporary home, and for the first two weeks, Kerouac achieved something truly rare in his life: happiness. With days that were cut down to the level of basic essentials—chopping wood for the stove, hiking, reading—Kerouac found what he needed to establish a kind of inner equilibrium. Appropriately, it seems, he read Robert Louis Stevenson's *Dr. Jekyll and Mr. Hyde* during this sabbatical and became obsessed with the sound of the ocean, making notes at night in an effort to duplicate, through language, this constant, rhythmic splash in the form of poems (which are included at the end of the book *Big Sur*). Eventually, of course, after the first two weeks had passed, Kerouac grew lonely, neurotic, and paranoid, terrified that he really didn't have any other writing left in him. He felt used up, and he was afraid that it was his own fault.

To escape this vortex of self-doubt, Kerouac evacuated the cabin and tried—mostly unsuccessfully—to hitch a ride back to town. Once there, he joined Whalen, Welch, a seventeen-year-old aspiring poet named Paul Smith, and a carnie, all of whom joined him on an extended drunk. Eventually, the group decided to head out to Ferlinghetti's cabin and continue the party there. On the way, Kerouac talked the group into stopping by the Cassadys' home. There, he rebuffed Carolyn's friendly affections, gruffly brought in Italian food and wine from a restaurant, and went with his friends to pick up Cassady from his tire-recapping gig when the work shift ended at two o'clock in the morning. And though the group continued on to the cabin, the Cassadys soon followed, as did Ferlinghetti himself, Whalen, an artist named Victor Wong, and the poet Michael McClure and his wife, Joanna. At one point McClure handed round a raunchy poem he'd written for Joanna which upset Carolyn, and although Kerouac loved and praised the poem, his own Achilles' Heel was soon exposed as he watched young Paul Smith make repeated attempts at seducing Carolyn; Kerouac fumed with anger, though Carolyn seemed utterly unresponsive and uninterested.

Upon leaving the cabin, Kerouac rode with Cassady, while Carolyn and Paul Smith caught a ride in another car. Cassady took this opportunity, being alone with his longtime friend, to tell Kerouac about a messy affair in which he was currently involved. The woman's name was Jackie Gibson, a mother of a four year old boy, and things had become complicated because she wanted Cassady to leave Carolyn for her—something he wouldn't do. Cassady, knowing his friend well (as well as knowing Kerouac's propensity to accept willingly Cassady's "seconds"), took him to meet Jackie, and shortly thereafter, she and Kerouac pursued a relationship.

Kerouac moved in almost immediately. The relationship began moving too fast for him, however, and Kerouac reached a stopping point when Jackie began harping on the idea of marriage. Rather than confronting her and being honest about his disinterest in marriage, however, Kerouac tried more passive-aggressive means to dissuade her on this point, including suggesting to her that she allow him to keep a mistress, and killing her son's goldfish by pouring red wine into its bowl. Neither venture worked, though, so Kerouac stewed up another idea, this one involving the Cassadys.

While traveling back to the cabin at Big Sur, accompanied by Jackie, her son, Lew Welch, and his girlfriend, Kerouac insisted that they stop in on the Cassadys, hoping somehow that the discomfort of Carolyn meeting Jackie would be intense enough to throw things off their current course. This failed, though, as the two women engaged in a polite conversation about child-rearing. Cassady, on the other hand, burned in anger, though the logical conclusion—that he was mad at Kerouac for bringing his former mistress into his home—didn't apply. No, Cassady was jealous of Kerouac's affair with Jackie, though he had not only suggested it but did what he could to put it into motion. Once again, Cassady had serious trouble living out, in real terms, what he theoretically believed in as a lifestyle.

Kerouac, meanwhile, would contend with his own form of madness later that night, unfortunately for all his guests. Having reached the cabin near Big Sur, he began hearing voices and grew paranoid—he believed he was in danger, and that his friends would try to poison him. Additionally, he hallucinated, hearing demons and seeing thick-winged bats flap around the cabin, until finally Kerouac had a religious vision, seeing Mary, angels, and Christ on the cross. Reportedly, Kerouac exclaimed in this moment, "I'm with you, Jesus, for always! Thank you!" as the vision faded; naturally, this unnerved everyone at the cabin, such that when Kerouac requested that Lew Welch drive him back into the city, he was only too ready to do so.

Soon, Kerouac was back in New York again, where he began to hang out with an artist (Stanley Twardowicz) who permitted Kerouac to watch him paint. Thus inspired, Kerouac registered for classes at the Actor's Studio, where both Marlon Brando and Marilyn Monroe were studying; typically, though, Kerouac didn't even make it through the first session. Another distraction soon arose in the form of a hallucinogenic drug, administered to Kerouac by the notoriously famous Timothy Leary—a Harvard professor who encouraged a generation of young people to, by way of LSD and other drugs, "tune in, turn on and drop out." Leary, particularly interested in how hallucinogenics affected the creative process of artists of different types, had a bad acid trip with Kerouac, who, according to Sandison, screamed at the scholar, "Can your drugs absolve the moral and venial sins which our beloved saviour, Jesus Christ, the only Son of God, came down and sacrificed his life upon the cross to wash away?" (145) To his credit, Kerouac walked away from these experiments; if nothing else remained of his Buddhism, he at least felt that he knew enlightenment was a slow, difficult process that had no shortcuts, chemical or otherwise.

But many young people disagreed, trying to "expand" their minds through drugs, and while Kerouac's own past drug use—most notably Benzadrine—would appear to place him in alignment with these young adults, he angrily chased them from his door when they made the pilgrimage to his home. Of course, many of these same people began protesting the Vietnam War, which annoyed Kerouac to no end. He considered himself to be extremely patriotic, and these young adults struck him as lazy—despite the fact that he rebelled against serving in the military himself. In the midst of his railing against the kids who showed up for a glimpse of the King of the Beats, though, Kerouac's health began to fail again in April 1961 (phlebitis, as usual), causing Gabrielle to urge her son to move with her to Florida. Nin and her husband lived near Orlando, so soon, Kerouac and Gabrielle traveled south and bought a home on Nin's street. When the move was complete, Kerouac journeyed to Mexico one last time to work on *Desolation Angels*, a novel that concentrated not only on his time on Desolation Peak, but also his adventures in New York, Tangier, and Mexico.

When Kerouac returned in June, he brought enough Benzadrine back to fuel a ten day writing spurt, the product of which was *Big Sur*. The novel re-traces Kerouac's doomed trip to Bixby Canyon, up to and including graphic details regarding his alcoholism and his mental breakdown. Ironically, though, Kerouac bought himself a case of cognac to celebrate the book's completion, demonstrating again the distance that perpetually existed between Kerouac's seemingly honest resolve and his lived life. He never managed to make the necessary connections between the two entities, connections that might have acted as a guide, had he heeded them. Instead, he went on a alcohol binge after finishing *Big Sur*, waking up in a haze in a hospital two weeks after he began drinking, and then he set off to New York to continue, drinking himself oblivious for another four weeks. Clearly, he was beyond anyone's help or control already, as Burroughs noted at this time; he treated Kerouac coolly, which naturally made Jack all the more depressed.

And things wouldn't get better from there. Kerouac was called into court, in the early part of 1962, to answer to Joan Haverty on the issue of child support for her ten year old daughter, Jan. The mother and daughter were living in extreme poverty at the time, and Kerouac's mandatory court appearance led to his first meeting with his daughter. Though paternity was never absolutely scientifically determined—despite positive blood tests, this was not considered wholly conclusive—most biographers agree that Jan bore a strong resemblance to Kerouac and that he was, in all likelihood, her biological father, despite Kerouac's protestations and claims about Joan's infidelity. Like her father, Jan would die at a relatively young age (44, from cancer) pursuant to a life of drugs, abuse, and prostitution, but where her father was concerned, she possessed a clear-eyed perspective, as shown by a comment she made on BBC Radio in 1987: "He had his own crazy reasons for not admitting that he was my father.... It was partly because he was busy being a baby himself, I think" (Sandison, 147). Indeed, though the court pressured Kerouac to pay at least minimal child support—fifty-two dollars and sixty-eight cents monthly—he refused, and years later, when Ginsberg reported to Kerouac the awful conditions of Jan and Joan's life on the streets, Kerouac turned a blind eye, never seeming to consider, even briefly, helping Jan to escape her circumstances. In this way, Kerouac seemed to transmit his own personal misery out to those who had briefly gotten close to him.

Hitting rock bottom, Kerouac, who had always romanticized his childhood, looked again to his hometown for comfort. A reinvigorated nostalgia fueled his trips to Lowell, but his old friends had matured and changed, finding the King of the Beats always too loud and too drunk to be around for very long. Striking out to find new friends, then, Kerouac made the acquaintance of a thiry-four-year old, zoot-suit-wearing Iroquois Indian named Paul Bourgeois. (Unfortunately, Bourgeois was a con man, and although he quickly convinced Kerouac that they were distantly related to each other, Nin and Gabrielle were much more suspicious upon meeting this slick character.) The two men went out drinking often, always on Kerouac's dollar, and they whooped and arm wrestled and spun daydreams about living on a reservation in the Arctic Circle. Although Kerouac would discover, a year later, that Bourgeois was a complete phony, he was the only friend he seemed to have at the time in Lowell.

And while one might expect the town, in general, to be at least somewhat proud of its famous son and make a fuss, the opposite appeared to be true; Kerouac's books seemed to promote an amorality that made the working class residents of the town uncomfortable, and most critics had dismissed the work as garbage anyway, so to say that no parade was ever planned around one of Kerouac's return trips to Lowell is to understate the deep embarrassment felt by this small, blue collar town regarding their King of the Beats. The closest that Kerouac got to recognition in Lowell while he lived was an invitation to be a guest on a radio show; Kerouac got drunk beforehand, though, of course, and murmured nonsense and wept throughout the course of the program. In a similar state, he went to see Stella Sampas, supposedly announcing his intentions to marry her, but she was horrified by the state of her old friend; she knew from his letters that he had problems with alcohol, but nothing could have prepared her for the bloated, sloppy mess of a man who stood hunched at her door.

Kerouac and Gabrielle soon moved back to Northport, Long Island, near Kerouac's old friend, Stanley Twardowicz, at the end of 1962. Twardowicz recalled that while walking the path between their houses, Kerouac often passed out, leaving the artist to look for Jack eventually and drag him back home to Gabrielle. Though a bit of an alcoholic herself, Gabrielle obviously held the reins in this home, and Kerouac put up little to no fight regarding her wishes. Indeed, when she barred Ginsberg from visiting Kerouac, her forty year old son protested not at all, making Ginsberg feel betrayed. But Gabrielle could not stop Kerouac from seeing Cassady one last time.

In late 1964, a group of drug-using hippies called the Merry Pranksters—led by writer Ken Kesey (*One Flew Over the Kuckoo's Nest*)—traveled across the country in a psychedelic, brightly-painted bus driven by Cassady. Chosen because of his caché as the real Dean Moriarty, Cassady had finally given up denying his identity, which he did for some time, and jumped on board, juggling sledgehammers on occasion to live up to his reckless, dangerous reputation. (Though he and Carolyn had divorced the year before, they remained on friendly terms.) Upon reaching New York, Cassady made a beeline for Kerouac, but once Jack met the Pranksters, who represented everything he thought had gone wrong recently with America's youth, his mood chilled considerably. To mention one example, nearly all Kerouac biographers mention an incident with an American flag that occurred during this get-together. The Pranksters had draped the flag over a couch in the Park Avenue apartment where they were staying and partying, but rather than sit on it, Kerouac pulled it off and carefully folded it. He also rejected many of the drugs on offer, though he accepted some marijuana and drank from his own whiskey. He seemed to stand apart, disapprovingly, though he reported to others that his reunion with Cassady had been a positive experience.

And though it probably didn't much affect his constant substance abuse, Kerouac, at this time, had more reasons than usual to drown his sorrows. He and Gabrielle, two months before, had moved to Florida again, only to be faced soon with Nin's tragic, unexpected death by heart attack in the Florida Sanitarium and Hospital in Orlando. Troubled by her separation from her husband, Paul, Nin had collapsed, in the end, upon getting a phone call from him; he had asked her for a divorce, telling her that he wished to marry someone else. And with Nin's passing, Gabrielle became the only family Kerouac had left. He and Gabrielle, though some comfort to each other, generally reinforced each other's alcoholism, and the two verbally sparred and bickered often, leaving Kerouac feeling emasculated and horribly depressed.

Also at this time, a group of young people, wearing jackets that read "Dharma Bums," traveled to Kerouac's Florida home as a kind of pilgrimage; reportedly, when this bloated, pathetic figure opened the door, all their faces fell, as if deflated, and Kerouac reported to a friend that this was one of the most depressing experiences of his life (Charters, 343). He also felt more and more isolated from his friends, who were willfully moving and pushing their way into the political spotlight. Whalen, Ginsberg, and Snyder were radicals who preached a new political consciousness and enlightenment; Kerouac, in sharp contrast, considered himself a staunchly conservative patriot who was simply a storyteller, not a spokesman. However, shortly after his reunion with Cassady, Kerouac finally got what seemed like good news: Grove Press wanted to fund Kerouac for a trip to France. For years, Kerouac had yearned for a project that would allow him to trace the ancestral lineage in which he took so much pride, and here, finally, was an opportunity to do just that.

As with all things at this time, though, Kerouac ruined his own best chances when he showed up in Paris' Bibliotheque National drunk and belligerent, demanding his family's records in joual, a dialect that surely left the staff baffled. Frustrated, and sure that these workers were deliberately conspiring to keep him away from information that was rightfully his, Kerouac sought solace in bars and among high-priced prostitutes. He soon moved on to Brittany to pursue his father Leo's roots, but instead of following this through, he did a sort of extended pub crawl, drinking with locals until it was time to go back to America.

Upon his return to Florida, he spent about a week writing *Satori in Paris* for Grove ("satori" meaning "a sudden illumination," or epiphany); in the book, Kerouac noted that a French cab driver provided him with a satori, and though Kerouac does not elaborate on what it was, he emphasizes that satori came from everyday small things; he also tells of his experience on a train, wherein he shared a compartment with a Catholic priest and an alcoholic traveler, and in the sense that satori should reveal one's true nature, he realized, in a moment of self-aware-ness, that these figures represented an externalization of his dual, conflicting natures. Despite this interesting observation, though, the book was published without fanfare, being slight in both quality and length.

During this period, Kerouac began spending a good deal of time in a bar frequented by the University of Southern Florida's students and faculty. Significantly, he made a point of ridiculing academics and picking fights with them; clearly, Kerouac felt threatened by them, and the reasons for this are important to con-sider. Because he had failed to finish college, while his friends Ginsberg and Burroughs, among others, had done graduate work, he harbored a deep-seated inferiority complex about his intel-lect—this despite the fact that given his personal reading habits, vocabulary, and discussions with others, he was a full-fledged intellectual. What seems to be at play here is Kerouac's apparent failure, in his own eyes, to live up to his mind's potential. He seemed obsessed by the idea that he had once had the capacity to be one of the academics he then so pointedly targeted; since he had not reached such heights, he tried to bring them down, in his own perspective, so as not to feel such intense, self-flagellating remorse. Not surprisingly, though, the strategy was ineffective and resulted in bar fights complete with cuts, bruises, and bone-breaks.

Hitting the road again, Kerouac headed back up north with Gabrielle, landing this time in Hyannis, on Cape Cod. That year, in 1966, a scholar named Ann Charters contacted him about com-piling a bibliography of his work. She traveled to meet Kerouac in his home, only to have her potential status as a Jew discussed by him and his mother in their variation of French, which Charters could nonetheless decode. In her biography, which was the first comprehensive one published on Kerouac, Charters noted the heated, constant bickering between Gabrielle and Kerouac, as though they were an embittered, old married couple. Both were drinking, and after Charters had spent the day there and was preparing to leave, Kerouac begged her to stay the night, threat-ening not to let her come back if she didn't. He backed down almost as soon as he voiced this desire, though, back-pedaling immediately, then he left to go to the bathroom. During this small window of opportunity, Gabrielle showed Charters a gash in the wall, where Kerouac had reportedly thrown a knife at her, and she urged Charters to leave. Not surprisingly, Charters followed this advice.

Sadly, Kerouac had become, in these last several years, so deeply entrenched in his alcoholism that every opportunity was wasted. He was asked to come to Rome, for instance, to celebrate the fact that a translation of *Big Sur* was slated to be the 500th publication for Arnoldo Mantadori. Drunk the whole time, he ruined two attempts at a television interview in Rome and was booed off the stage in Naples for defending America's intervention in Vietnam. Of course, in order to leave the stage, or walk at all, he needed help, since he then seemed incapable of even basic mobility. He returned to America in this condition, and things were fated to get even worse: Gabrielle suffered a stroke, which made her even more dependent on a son who clearly couldn't even take care of himself.

CHAPTER SEVEN

The Beat Goes On

*It was a soul understanding that Jack and I had
that everybody had to be tender towards each other
because you were only in your own one place very
briefly, in a sense ghosts because so transient, every-
body lost in a dream world of their own making.
Really a kind of farewell dream. We talked about
that a lot and that really was the basis of the Beat
Generation, the poignant kewpee-doll dearness of
personages vanishing in time.*

—Allen Ginsberg, qtd. in *Jack Kerouac
King of the Beats: A Portrait*

AS HE OFTEN DID, Kerouac turned his thoughts back to his hometown and his childhood, and the answer he came back to was
Stella Sampas, his dear friend Sammy's older sister. She had never
left Lowell, and had never married, so Kerouac's bid for her hand
was successful, and they married in Novemeber 1966. Kerouac's
many biographers, for the most part, agree that this marriage was
solely a pragmatic one; in Stella—by conventional standards, a
plain, unattractive woman—Kerouac sought and found a free
nursemaid for Gabrielle, as well as someone to fill the hole left by
Gabrielle in terms of taking care of him. Apparently, Stella

assumed these roles without complaint, as Kerouac must have known she would.

Taking his nostalgia to new heights, Kerouac also tried to buy the house in which Gerard had died, but this fell through and other arrangements were made. The three moved into a large house in Lowell, and Kerouac tried to resume work on *Vanity of Duluoz*, a novel that recounted his football-fueled move from Lowell to New York in the spring of 1967. Significantly, in one Canadian television interview given at this time, when prompted with a question about what in modern life makes him sick, Kerouac said, "I'm sick of myself" (Amburn, 359); more encouragingly, however, Kerouac was interviewed in the *Paris Review* in its "Art of Fiction" series. He was being credited for inspiring, through his personal, confessional style, the New Journalism, wherein reporters subjectively narrated the story, deliberately working themselves into it rather than remaining invisible and striving to maintain objectivity.

Despite this mark of distinction, though, Kerouac found himself more often at the bar in Lowell instead of in front of the typewriter—specifically, a bar owned by Stella's brother, Nicky Sampas. Though Nicky let Kerouac run his mouth, including slurs against Stella, he drew the line when Kerouac brought hookers into the bar with him. When thus ejected, Kerouac and his paid escort would find a different place, and then he would come home and play jazz records until sun-up. In the midst of this hedonistic routine, Kerouac got a surprise visit from Jan, his daughter by Joan Haverty, in November. Surprisingly, Kerouac, on this one occasion, seemed glad to see her, though the pregnant fifteen year old—with a pony-tailed boyfriend in tow—had to shout to him over the noise of *The Beverly Hillbillies* playing on the television. Nonetheless, she got his blessing to use his name, as well as positive reinforcement regarding her plan to leave for Mexico and write. (Gabrielle, never wholly recovering from her stroke, mistook Jan for Nin, asking for her from her wheelchair.)

On the heels of the publication of *Vanity of Duluoz* in February 1968, Kerouac learned that his original human muse, Neal Cassady, had died, likely due to some kind of overdose, lying next to railroad tracks in Mexico. On some level, Kerouac couldn't process this loss, expecting Cassady to show up any minute and prove the story wrong; but of course, he never did. In an attempt to snap Jack from his blues, Stella's brothers, Nick and Tony, planned to take him on a trip through Europe, stopping in Spain, Portugal, Switzerland, and Germany. Disturbingly, biographer and editor Ellis Amburn reported that Kerouac, before leaving on this trip, phoned to say that he was off "to see the concentration camps, and dance on Jews' graves" (363). (Though many discredit this account, Amburn mantains Kerouac still harbored an intense anti-Semitism, drawn from his parents, his hometown, and Father Caughlin's weekly propagandistic radio shows.) Kerouac was ultimately disappointed by the trip, however; though he had respected the Germans and their ideals during World War II, he quickly became disenchanted upon meeting them in person. Again, he drank himself into a stupor that lasted throughout the trip, finding and hiring prostitutes to sneak into his room, and cried nearly constantly. Yet another opportunity had passed him by, and the fault lay in his alcoholism.

After Kerouac's return, he was scheduled to appear on conservative pundit William F. Buckley's television show, *Firing Line*. Given Kerouac's conservative leanings, he very much respected this man who had become an articulate, mass media mouthpiece for the right. Not that this was evident from Kerouac's appearance on the debate show. Slurring his words, drunk again, Kerouac was mostly incoherent, struggling hard to define the Beats' ideology, as well as to explain how his Catholicism worked with, rather than contradicted, this belief system. Ginsberg sat in the audience, and after the show had begun, its producers approached him, begging him to take Kerouac's place on the panel. Knowing his old friend as he did, however, Ginsberg refused, aware that this would further damage Kerouac's already-shrunken, fragile ego. Ginsberg was almost never one to shun the limelight, but his loyalty to Kerouac won out on this occasion, and as it happened, this night was the last time he would see Kerouac alive.

In September 1968, Gabrielle pressured Kerouac to move to

Florida again to avoid the cold winter, so they headed to St. Petersburg, funded by the sale of Kerouac's correspondence to Ginsberg to Columbia's archives. Once there, Kerouac struggled to work on a project he started long ago, called *Pic*. Similar to *On the Road*, this novel narrated adventures from the perspective of a black farm worker named Pictorial Review Jackson. (Published posthumously, most critics agreed that Kerouac's attempts at capturing black dialect were misguided.) Still disenchanted with others' interpretation of his past work, however, he grumbled after seeing *Easy Rider*, remarking, apparently with no sense of hypocrisy, "Neal and I had a hell of a good time, and we didn't hurt anybody. They're trying to make heroes out of those guys, and they're not heroes. They're criminals" (Amburn, 369).

While pursuing this final project, Kerouac was approached by a reporter from the *Miami Herald*, Jack McClintock, who noted that as he sat in near darkness, in a room that had pictures of the Pope and Gerard (a significant pairing), Kerouac railed against "Communists, hippies, and the 'Jewish literary mafia'" while also blaming the excesses of Ken Kesey for Neal Cassady's early demise (Sandison, 156). Each day, meanwhile, he and Stella and Gabrielle lived a penurious existence; he hoped to see a royalty check in the mail, though none came, and Stella wore sleeveless muumuus, with Jack's old T-shirts underneath, and caught the bus to her job, where she hunched over a sewing machine all day. Feeling isolated and lonely again, Kerouac tried calling Carolyn Cassady once, out in California, at four o'clock in the morning. Not in the mood to talk just then—particularly since Kerouac was, as usual, drunk, and she had been out late at a party—she acted as though the connection was bad and she couldn't hear him. Kerouac tried, again and again, to call, and each time she told the same story. She had no idea, of course, that this would be the last time she might talk to him, and that she was the recipient of one of Jack's last, flailing attempts to connect with his friends.

In late October of that year, when Kerouac was forty-seven years old, he suddenly felt nauseous and experienced bad cramps while watching *The Galloping Gourmet* on television. (Some scholars surmise that a recent, late-night bar-fight had set these physical events in motion.) He vomited blood, and although he was rushed to the hospital, operated on for several hours, and given twenty-six transfusions (many of which his body seemed to reject), he died of a hemorrhage the next day, on October 21, 1969. Kerouac's death certificate explains the cause as "gastrointestinal hemorrhage, due to bleeding gastric varix from cirrhosis of liver, due to excessive ethanol intake many years" (Amburn, 373). He'd finally drunk himself to death, and the news slowly spread. Walter Cronkite announced it on the national news; in upstate New York, Corso and Ginsberg, upon learning of Jack's death, went for a walk and carved their friend's name in a tree; Carolyn, angered by being so far away when Jack died, just as she had been when Cassady died, ultimately decided that the distance was actually a blessing in disguise, allowing her to keep both men alive in her memory; and Kerouac's boyhood friends tied one on at the bowling alley in Lowell, where Leo had once worked.

Throughout his career, of course, Kerouac had often contemplated and written about death; this passage from *The Subterraneans*, for example, demonstrates how his ghostly cognizance of death's inevitability affected his worldview:

> now death bends big wings over my window, I see it, I hear it, I smell it, I see it in the limp hang of my shirts destined to be not worn, new-old, stylish-out-of-date, neckties snakelike behung I don't even use any more, new blankets for autumn peace beds now writhing rushing cots on the sea of self-murder—

In this moment, Kerouac's constant awareness regarding mortality—which perpetually colored his perspective, including the mundane items of his everyday life (in this instance, clothing and linens)—saturates much of his prose, reminding readers that tangible, man-made possessions, the things we simply use and forget on a day to day basis for our various needs, will remain long after the user's life extinguishes. In another passage from the same novel, Kerouac raises the specter of spiritual complexities in relation to death, as voiced by Adele Lee's character, Mardou Fox:

Why should anyone want to harm my little heart, my feet, my little hands, my skin that I'm wrapt in because God wants me warm and Inside, my toes—why did God make all this all so decayable and dieable and harmable and wants to make me realize and scream—why the wild ground and bodies bare and breaks—I quaked when the giver creamed, when my father screamed, my mother dreamed—I started small and ballooned up and now I'm big and a naked child again and only to cry and fear.—Ah—Protect yourself, angel of no harm, you who've never and could never harm and crack another innocent its shell and thin veiled pain— wrap a robe around you, honey lamb, protect yourself from rain and wait, till Daddy comes again, and Mama throws you warm inside her valley of the moon, loom at the loom of patient time, be happy in the mornings. (26)

Though a Catholic who strove to adopt Buddhist ideals and philosophies, Kerouac never appeared to find comfort in the idea of death. Instead, the kind of tense, puzzled wonder exhibited in this passage, regarding the seeming hypocrisies of a Creator, or God, who generously gives only to take away, seems more prevalent. Gerard's death taught Kerouac early on that death could come at any time, and that there was often no rhyme nor reason involved; when Kerouac's own death seemed to occur so suddenly, despite the abuse he'd heaped upon his own body for years on end, Kerouac's friends, his wife, and his mother were likely confronted by the same sorts of confusions, shock, and frustrations.

Though an open-casket service occurred in St. Petersburg shortly after Kerouac's death, Stella and Gabrielle sent his remains to Lowell for a wake; one hundred mourners came to see Kerouac one last time there, laid out in a brown-checked blazer and a red bow tie. Father Morrisette, the man who first encouraged Kerouac to write, as well as to seek a college scholarship through football, presided over the funeral service, which was attended by the Sampas family; Allen Ginsberg; Peter Orlovsky; Gregory Corso; John Clellen Holmes and his wife, Shirley; Ann and Sam Charters; Edie Parker (who strangely introduced herself as Mrs. Jack Kerouac); and Sterling Lord, Kerouac's agent. (Burroughs was in

London and did not return for the funeral.) And while this turnout was a boon, in terms of being a Beat Generation who's who list, Kerouac's death seemed to happen quietly, with little fanfare or discussion—all Kerouac's books were then out of print—though Gabrielle wailed upon seeing her son in a casket, calling him "pretty" and "my little boy."

Ginsberg, Corso, and Orlovsky approached the casket, their arms linked, and Ginsberg reportedly thought about how Kerouac resembled Buddha: he came to Earth, delivered his message, and simply, suddenly left it. As part of the service, Ginsberg read a few of Kerouac's poems from *Mexico City Blues*; later, however, Stella approached Corso to scold him for fading away from Jack's life, then turned this same accusation upon them all. She eventually calmed down, and Kerouac's body was ultimately laid to rest in Lowell, next to Sammy (against Kerouac's wishes; he had specifically told Stella, repeatedly, that he wished to be buried near his father in Nashua, New Hampshire). Local Catholic leaders had protested Kerouac's burial in a Catholic cemetery, grousing because of the author's apparent preaching of immorality to the masses, but Father Morrissette won the day.

And although his estate at that time seemed paltry, Stella continued to care for Gabrielle until the old woman died four years later. And soon, to her surprise, Kerouac's work enjoyed a kind of resurrection. As with many artists who came before him, Kerouac received more glory in death than he ever had in life. With new, more zealous interest, academics, students, and disenfranchised young people found their way to Kerouac again, gaining a hope and sense of community that Kerouac himself never fully enjoyed.

Ginsberg had once told Ann Charters that Kerouac's books concerned themselves with "mortal souls wandering earth in time that is vanishing under our feet," (65) but this now seems a heartbreaking description of the author himself. For although many will continue to find much to dislike in the lived life of the man—in terms of his oft-reported racism, misogyny, homophobia, and selfishness—Kerouac's readers nonetheless never fail to be awed by the far-reaching, never-ending positive impact his work has had on American culture and society. In the wake of his words—his stream-of-chaotic-consciousness—the ideals of emotional honesty, compassion, and open-mindedness were felt by millions of readers, even though the messenger never quite seemed to get his own story straight.

SOMETIMES IT'S EASY to forget that there was a human being—a flawed, shy, miserable man—behind the industry that has, in recent decades, become Jack Kerouac's legend and image. Lowell's minor league baseball team, the Spinners, recently had a Jack Kerouac Bobblehead Night in order to attract spectators to a game; the rock band 10,000 Maniacs, fronted by then-lead singer Natalie Merchant, sang an enconium called "Hey Jack Kerouac"; just a few years ago, GAP used a photo of the author in print ads with the tag line, "Kerouac wore khakis"; And recently, Kerouac's correspondence with the young woman he had an affair with when *On the Road* was released—Joyce (Glassman) Johnson—was adapted for the stage. Kerouac's image (as a young man, usually, rather than as a bloated middle-aged drunk, in the tradition of Elvis) regularly appears on t-shirts, posters, coffee mugs, and tote bags. Given Kerouac's ideological rejection of American hyper-consumerism, the bobblehead doll, among these other items for sale, would likely depress him and strike him as gaudily capitalist—the tangible antithesis of what he wished to achieve. However, while Kerouac has been reduced to a monolithic symbol by many of these efforts, made into a palatable mainstream product that speaks to a limited number of associations and ideals—per the media's shorthand constructions of Elvis Presley, Marilyn Monroe, Malcolm X, JFK, Albert Einstein, and James Dean—the fact still remains that in order to inspire such a wave of sustained interest and engagement, Kerouac must have spoken to some need, desire, and anxiety that was quintessentially American.

For indeed, what anxieties are more American than the perpetual interior battle between cynicism and optimism, anarchy and control, freedom and security, hubris and self-doubt, and individuality and belonging that readers witness again and again in Kerouac's work? At the outset of *The Subterraneans*, the exuberant flood of ideas which defined Kerouac's style sets the tone and threatens to drown readers while simultaneously exhilerating them, a Kerouac trademark:

> Once I was young and had so much more orientation and could talk with nervous intelligence about everything and with clarity and without as much literary preambling as this; in other words this is the story of an unself-confident man, at the same time of an egomaniac, naturally, facetious won't do—just to start at the beginning and let the truth seep out, that's what I'll do—

And while the truth that escaped him was necessarily subjective, screened through Kerouac's specific, experience-molded lens, it nonetheless has produced much that is positive in our current culture, and for this, we must be grateful. Our culture chooses to remember him for his contributions rather than for his flaws. Kerouac affected the trajectory of American culture inalterably, paying the price of an unhappy, prematurely short life, a life in which he never really felt comfortable, wanting to always be where he was not.

Of course, one of the most central, most fascinating components of the Kerouac story is how much he disliked feeling as though no one understood him, despite the fact that all of his fictional work exposed the bulk of his remembered life.

Presciently, at age twenty-three, Kerouac wrote a short novel (published only after his death) called *Orpheus Emerged*; the story, which focused on a group of young, free-thinking intellectuals attending college in New York City, dealt with the impossibility of acting and living a real life, according to the strict tenets of a theoretical ideal. One character in the novel struggles, for instance, while standing on a bridge alone one night. The ideological truths he holds dear dictate that he should jump and commit suicide.

But all that can't be foreseen or taken into account by theory—human emotion as well as the capacities for both good and evil—comes into play, and rather than simply acting out of ideological if/then statements (think of Neal, who pushed his women onto Kerouac because of the "New Vision" ideals, despite the fact that he always became furiously jealous), the young man pauses and is brought back from the brink, back to the circle of his friends. And while Kerouac might have been recovered by friends and human reality, too, had he lived long enough, he seemed, at the time of his death, to be still striving to force his life into the incompatible, impossible image of Gerard and Neal—not to mention the "New Vision" of Ginsberg and Carr—a quest he was forever destined to fail.

Nonetheless, Kerouac used the medium of writing to provide himself with a public confessional, and he did so with the passion and fury of a young man possessed, eager to lighten his load. The irony, however, was that his baggage only got heavier when he published and, as a consequence, lost control of his image in the public sphere. Despite the fact that an inordinately high number of Kerouac biographies are available, and many of the myths surrounding the writer have long ago been de-bunked, a resistance to reality persists in regard to the writer. Americans, it would seem, want the myth in the bobbleheaded form of plastic and mounted springs; the young, enthusiastic frozen moment in time that is the heart of *On the Road*; the black and white book cover image of a young, carefree, handsome loner, leaning back against a car, ready to drop everything (and everyone) just for the sake of going. With this in mind, Kerouac's stock image seems the epitome of irony: the man who desperately strove, again and again, to simplify his own life—stripping it down to its most basic essentials, per Thoreau and Buddhist teachings—has had it permanently, erroneously simplified for him.

Amburn, Ellis. *Subterranean Kerouac: The Hidden Life of Jack Kerouac.* New York: St. Martin's Press, 1998.

Charters, Ann. *Kerouac: A Biography.* San Francisco: Straight Arrow, 1973.

———, ed. *Jack Kerouac: Selected Letters: 1940–1956.* New York: Viking, 1995.

———, ed. *The Portable Jack Kerouac.* New York: Viking, 1995.

Clark, Tom. *Jack Kerouac.* New York: Paragon House, 1984.

Gifford, Barry and Lawrence Lee. *Jack's Book: An Oral Biography of Jack Kerouac.* New York: St. Martin's Press, 1978.

Kerouac, Jack. *On the Road.* New York: Penguin Books USA Inc., 1991.

———*The Subterraneans.* New York: Grove Press, 1958.

———*Visions of Gerard.* New York: Penguin Books USA Inc., 1987.

McNally, Dennis. *Desolate Angel: Jack Kerouac, the Beat Generation, and America.* New York: Random House, 1979.

Miles, Barry. *Jack Kerouac King of the Beats: A Portrait.* London: Virgin Publishing Ltd., 1998.

Nicosia, Gerald. *Memory Babe.* Berkeley: University of California Press, 1983.

Sandison, David. *Jack Kerouac: An Illustrated Biography.* Chicago: Chicago Review Press, Incorporated, 1999.

1922	Jean-Louis Lebris de Kerouac is born on March 12, 1922 at 5:00 P.M. in Lowell, MA. Son of Gabrielle (L'Evesque) and Leo Kerouac, brother to Gerard, age 5, and Caroline (Nin), age 3.
1923	Leo opens Spotlight Print in Lowell.
1926	Brother Gerard dies of rheumatic fever at age 9.
1933	Jack skips sixth grade and begins school at Bartlett Junior High School, where he first befriends Sebastian "Sammy" Sampas and writes his first short story in nickel notebooks.
1936	Flood ravages the town of Lowell, and although Spotlight Print is only marginally damaged, Leo's finances are so precarious that this puts him out of business; Kerouac, having formed teams with his friends, begins to recognize his skill in running, baseball, and football, with the latter being his strongest sport.
1939	Graduates from high school, then, in the fall, heads to Horace Mann, a private high school in New York that is intended to fill in academic gaps for Kerouac before he enters Columbia to play on a football scholarship.
1940	Graduates from Horace Mann, though he can't attend the ceremony as he can not afford the required garb, and he starts classes at Columbia; on the football field, he's quickly injured, and he starts cutting classes, pursuing his own study interests.
1941	Gets upset with Columbia football coach Lou Little because Kerouac will not start, and he leaves the team, taking a trip to Washington D.C. before heading back to his parents' home.
1942–43	Serves in the Merchant Marine on the *S.S. Dorchester*, heading for Greenland, then joins the Navy in February; after a short time in boot camp, Kerouac revolts against the binding rules and is later discharged as schizophrenic; on the *S.S. George Weems*, Kerouac sails as a merchant marine once more, heading to Liverpool, and upon his

return, he hangs out with Edie Parker, at the apartment she shares with Joan Vollmer, and meets Edie's new friend, Lucien Carr.

1944 Through Lucien Carr, who becomes close friends with Kerouac, he meets William Burroughs and Allen Ginsberg; Sammy Sampas is killed in the war; Carr kills his longtime older admirer, David Kammerer, and seeks advice from Burroughs, then help from Kerouac, who aids him in disposing of evidence before Carr goes to the police; because of his actions, Kerouac is arrested, and he agrees to marry Edie in order to get her family to pay for his bail; a salon among the friends forms, wherein Kerouac, Ginsberg, Burroughs, Parker, and Vollmer share a New York apartment on W. 115th St.

1945 Kerouac writes *Orpheus Emerged*, a novella that was only published posthumously in 2000, and co-authors with Burroughs a novel about Kammerer's murder called *And the Hippos Were Boiled in Their Tanks*, which has never been published; near the end of the year, Kerouac is hospitalized for clots in his legs, which developed as a result of his excessive Benzadrine use.

1946 Leo Kerouac dies of cancer, which fuels Kerouac's efforts to write the novel, *The Town and the City*; he meets Neal Cassady, whose letters (to Hal Chase) Kerouac had read and admired; his marriage to Edie is annulled.

1947 Travels, in hopes of a job on a ship embarking from California, and with Gabrielle's help, to Denver, where he sees Cassady occasionally; he also meets Neal's new mistress, Carolyn Robinson, a theater studies graduate student who would later marry Neal; Kerouac continues on to California, but fails to find work on a ship; he gets another job as a security guard, but he returns to New York in the fall.

1948 Meets John Clellen Holmes, finishes *The Town and the City*, and works on the first attempts at *On the Road*.

1949	Takes another cross-country journey with Cassady, Cassidy's first wife LuAnne Henderson, and a friend named Al Hinkle after they show up at Nin's home in North Carolina at Christmastime; Cassady deserts LuAnne and Kerouac in California, driving off to re-unite with Carolyn; Kerouac has a brief affair with LuAnne, makes up with Neal, then heads back to Nin's house; Harcourt-Brace accepts *The Town and the City* for publication, giving Kerouac a $1000 advance, which he uses to move to Denver.
1950	Kerouac's first novel is published with lukewarm to positive reviews, but it is so much in the tradition of Thomas Wolfe that it quickly falls off the literary radar; he drives to Mexico with Cassady, who leaves Kerouac to visit Burroughs and Joan by himself; after making his way back to New York, Kerouac meets Joan Haverty and is married to her after two weeks time.
1951	In April, Kerouac writes, in a coffee-fueled three week spurt, the first complete draft of *On the Road* on a teletype roll, in one run-on paragraph; his marriage with Joan breaks up when she tells him she's pregnant and not only refuses to get an abortion but also insists that it's his child; he develops a method of writing he calls "sketching," which leads him to start writing an expanded version of *On the Road* called *Visions of Cody*; moves to Neal and Carolyn Cassady's home in San Francisco in December.
1952	Works on *Visions of Cody* in San Francisco, then *Dr. Sax* while in Mexico; comes back to San Francisco, where he works as a brakeman and pursues a discreet, though Neal-encouraged, affair with Carolyn before he leaves the Cassadys' home and writes one of his most famous essays, "October on the Railroad Earth"; Goes to Mexico again, then back to New York, where Joan Haverty has given birth to Jan Kerouac alone.
1953	Writes *Maggie Cassidy* in New York before heading out west again to work for the railroad in San Jose; obtains

work as a waiter on the *William Carruth* but goes AWOL almost immediately, in Alabama, where he is found drunk with a hooker; he leaves the ship in New Orleans, then heads back to New York, where he begins an affair with Alene Lee, an African American woman, and writes *The Subterraneans*, which focuses on their affair, in a three day spurt of writing; (Also writes "The Essentials of Spontaneous Prose" to articulate his writing method); the couple breaks up soon thereafter.

1954   Pursues the study of Buddhism in New York and California, moving to Neal and Carolyn's place in San Jose; writes poetry collection *San Francisco Blues* and begins taking notes on his translations and observations regarding Buddhism, calling the project *Some of the Dharma*, with the initial intention of pursuing the project for Ginsberg's edification; Kerouac obtains an agent, Sterling Lord, but then is called to court for failing to pay child support to Joan Haverty.

1955   After traveling to Mexico City again, falls for a drug-dealing prostitute named Esperanza Villanueva; he begins to write a book about their affair, *Tristessa*, as well as a book of poems called *Mexico City Blues*, which largely stems from his conversations with Burroughs' old friend Billy Garver while stoned; Kerouac heads to California to see Ginsberg, who's planning the now-famous Six Gallery reading, working on "Howl," and becoming a mainstay of the San Francisco literary scene, which includes figures like Gary Snyder, Philip Whalen, Michael McClure, Kenneth Rexroth, and Lawrence Ferlinghetti; after "Howl" is read publicly for the first time, Kerouac hikes with Snyder for a few days, and then heads to Nin's home in North Carolina.

1956   Writes *Visions of Gerard*, an enconium to his brother, and writes a letter to attain a position as a fire marshal in Washington State; he goes to California again, sharing Gary Snyder's cabin while writing *Scripture of the Golden*

Eternity and *Old Angel Midnight*; after hitchhiking his way up the coast, Kerouac is trained as a fire marshal, then is left in isolation in a lookout tower for six weeks; when the shift ends, Kerouac heads to Mexico again, where he begins work on *Desolation Angels* and completes *Tristessa; On the Road* is finally accepted by Viking, after a number of articles about the Beats make them hot commodities; Kerouac returns to New York.

1957	Travels to Tangier, Morocco, where Burroughs had lived for two years, and then goes on to Europe; upon his return, tries at first to move his mother to Berkeley, California, but they soon end up heading to Orlando, Florida; goes back to New York and begins a romance with Joyce Glassman just before *On the Road* is published; while reviews are mixed, the *New York Times* features a rave review; writes a book about his hiking trip with Snyder, calling it *The Dharma Bums*.
1958	Grove Press publishes *The Subterraneans*, which is panned by critics, and Viking publishes *The Dharma Bums*; buys a house in Northport, Long Island, and moves his mother into it; begins affair with artist Dody Muller.
1959	Collaborates on a film project, inspired by one act of a play he wrote, called *Pull My Daisy; Dr. Sax* and *Mexico City Blues*; published by Grove and *Maggie Cassidy* published by Avon; sells the house in Northport and heads back to Orlando, only to return to Northport with her again shortly thereafter; Attends premiere of *Pull My Daisy* in San Francisco, appears on *The Steve Allen Show*, and drives back to New York with friends Lew Welch and Albert Saijo.
1960	Onslaught of Kerouac titles on the market continues: Avon publishes *Tristessa*; Amiri Baraka's Totem Press publishes *Scripture of the Golden Eternity*, New Directions publishes *Visions of Cody*; McGraw-Hill publishes the essay collection *Lonesome Traveler*, and Ferlinghetti's outfit, City Lights, plans to publish *Book of Dreams;*

Kerouac heads out to San Francisco by train to write in a remote cabin near Big Sur, owned by Ferlinghetti, and demands complete secrecy, but when he arrives, he goes on an extended pub crawl, alerting everyone in town to his presence; he suffers a breakdown while at the cabin, then returns to his mother in Northport.

1961   Tries LSD with Ginsberg and Harvard professor Timothy Leary but has a bad experience; moves Gabrielle back to Florida, then heads to Mexico, where he works on *Desolation Angels*; he returns to Florida, where he writes— in a ten day writing spurt—about his alcoholism and mental breakdown in California, calling the novel *Big Sur*; back in New York, he parties with Lucien Carr and others.

1962   Travels all over the East Coast: Florida, New York, Maine, Cape Cod, Connecticut, Massachusetts; Farrar, Strauss, and Cudahy publishes *Big Sur*, and Kerouac moves with his mother back up to Northport.

1963   Farrar, Strauss, and Cudahy publish *Visions of Gerard*.

1964   Cassady rolls into town driving the Merry Pranksters' bus; retrieving Kerouac, Cassady brings him to a Merry Pranksters party on Park Avenue, but Kerouac is less than impressed with them; He writes *Vanity of Duluoz* and moves his mother to St. Petersburg, Florida; Nin dies unexpectedly from a heart attack.

1965   Coward-McCann publishes *Desolation Angels*, and Grove Press gives him the money, and the opportunity, to visit France and perform research on his ancestors and heritage; he spends the trip drinking and whoring and returns to Florida, where he writes *Satori in Paris* in a week; he spends a good deal of time at a University of Southern Florida hangout, belittling academics, then goes to his hometown of Lowell for a visit.

1966   Moves mother to Hyannis, on Cape Cod, where she soon suffers a stroke; Grove publishes the ill-received *Satori in Paris*, and he travels to Italy, by invitation, to celebrate the publication of *Big Sur*, he is so drunk that he can barely stand, however, and he is booed from an event after defending American intervention in Vietnam; after his return, he proposes to Sammy Sampas' sister, Stella, and they marry, though it's clearly a pragmatic arrangement.

1967	Moves Gabrielle to Lowell with Stella, and he quickly becomes a regular at Nicky's Bar, a pub owned by Stella's brother; writes *Vanity of Duluoz*; his daughter, Jan, comes by, unannounced and pregnant, heading to Mexico with her boyfriend; Kerouac encourages her to go there and write and tells her she can use his name.
1968	In Mexico, Cassady dies (seemingly of an overdose) lying next to railroad tracks; *Vanity of Duluoz* is published, and Kerouac travels with Stella's brothers Tony and Nick to Europe; again, he spends the whole trip drinking and whoring; he appears on William F. Buckley's *Firing Line* television show, but he is incoherent and drunk; he and Stella move Gabrielle to Florida yet again, landing in St. Petersburg for the last time.
1969	Feeling nauseous one day in October, Kerouac goes to the bathroom and vomits blood; after a day in the hospital, and many attempts at blood transfusions, he dies at the age of forty-seven; there is an open casket funeral in St. Petersburg, but Gabrielle and Stella have his remains sent to Lowell for a wake, which is attended by one hundred mourners, including Ginsberg, Corso, and Orlovsky; Kerouac is buried in Lowell, though his express wishes, voiced to Stella, were that he wished to be buried in Nashua, New Hampshire, next to his father.

The Town and the City (1950)

On the Road (1957)

The Subterraneans (1958)

The Dharma Bums (1958)

Dr. Sax (1959)

Maggie Cassidy (1959)

Mexico City Blues (1959)

Abridged version of *Visions of Cody* (1959)

The Scripture of the Golden Eternity (1960)

Tristessa (1960)

Lonesome Traveler (1960)

A long form poem titled *Rimbaud* (1960)

Book of Dreams (1961)

Screenplay for *Pull My Daisy* (1961)

Big Sur (1962)

Visions of Gerard (1963)

Desolation Angels (1965)

Sartori in Paris (1966)

Vanity of Duluoz: An Adventurous Education, 1935–46 (1968)

POSTHUMOUS PUBLICATIONS:

Scattered Poems (compiled by Ann Charters) (1971)

Pic (1971)

Visions of Cody (1973)

Trip Trap: Haiku Along the Road from San Francisco to New York 1959 (with Albert Saijo and Lew Welch) (1973)

Two Early Stories (1973)

Heaven and Other Poems (edited by Don Allen) (1977)

Take Care of My Ghost, Ghost (with Allen Ginsberg) (1977)

Pomes All Sizes (1992)

Old Angel Midnight (edited by Don Allen) (1993)

Good Blonde and Others (1993)

Book of Blues (1995)

The Portable Jack Kerouac (edited by Ann Charters) (1995)

San Francisco Blues (1995)

Selected Letters: 1940–1956 (edited by Ann Charters) (1995)

Some of the Dharma (1997)

Atop an Underwood: Early Stories and Other Writings (1999)

Selected Letters: 1957–1969 (1999)

Orpheus Emerged (2000)

Door Wide Open: A Beat Affair in Letters, 1957–58 (with Joyce Johnson) (2000)

Beaulieu, Victor-Levy (translated by Sheila Fischman). *Jack Kerouac: A Chicken Essay.* Toronto: Coach House Press, 1975.

Bloom, Harold, ed. *Modern Critical Interpretations:* On the Road. Philadelphia: Chelsea House Publishers, 2004.

Cassady, Carolyn. *Heart Beat: My Life with Jack and Neal.* Berkeley: Creative Arts Book Company, 1976.

———. *Off the Road: My Years with Cassady, Kerouac, and Ginsberg.* New York: Penguin, 1991.

Cassady, Neal. *The First Third.* San Francisco: City Lights, 1971.

Charters, Ann. *A Bibliography of Works by Jack Kerouac.* New York: Phoenix Bookshop, 1975.

———. *The Portable Beat Reader.* New York: Viking Press, 1992.

———. *The Portable Kerouac Reader.* New York: Viking Press, 1995.

Christy, Jim. *The Long Slow Death of Jack Kerouac.* Toronto: ECW Press, 1998.

Cook, Bruce. *The Beat Generation.* New York: Scribner's, 1971.

Dorfner, John J. *Kerouac: Visions of Lowell.* Raleigh, NC: Cooper Street Publications, 1993.

French, Warren. *Jack Kerouac.* Boston: Twayne, 1986.

George-Warren, Holly, editor. *The Rolling Stone Book of the Beats: The Beat Generation and American Culture.* New York: Hyperion, 1999.

Holmes, John Clellon. *Go!* New York: New American Library, 1980.

Hunt, Tim. *Kerouac's Crooked Road: Development of a Fiction.* Hamden, CT: Archon, 1981.

Jarvis, Charles E. *Visions of Kerouac.* Lowell, MA: Ithaca Press, 1974.

Johnson, Joyce. *Minor Characters: A Young Woman's Coming of Age in the Beat Orbit of Jack Kerouac.* New York: Penguin, 1999.

Johnson, Joyce and Jack Kerouac. *Door Wide Open: A Beat Love Affair in Letters, 1957–58.* New York: Viking Press, 2000.

Jones, Jim. *Use My Name: Jack Kerouac's Forgotten Families.* Toronto: ECW Press, 1999.

Jones, James T. *Jack Kerouac's Duluoz Legend: The Mythic Form of an Autobiographical Fiction.* Southern Illinois Press, 1999.

Kerouac, Jan. *Baby Driver: A Story About Myself.* New York: St. Martin's Press, 1981.

———. *Trainsong.* New York: Henry Holt, 1988.

McClure, Michael. *Scratching the Beat Surface.* San Francisco: North Point, 1982.

McDarrah, Fred. *Kerouac and Friends: A Beat Generation Album.* New York: Morrow, 1984.

Montgomery, John: *Kerouac West Coast.* Palo Alto, CA: Fels and Firn, 1976.

———. *Kerouac at the "Wild Boar."* San Anselmo: Fels and Firn Press, 1986.

Morgan, Bill. *The Beat Generation in New York: A Walking Tour of Jack Kerouac's City.* San Francisco: City Lights, 1997.

Parker, Brad. *Kerouac: An Introduction.* Lowell Corporation for the Humanities, 1989.

Theado, Matt. *Understanding Jack Kerouac.* Columbia, SC: University of South Carolina Press, 2000.

Turner, Steve. *Angelheaded Hipster: A Life of Jack Kerouac.* New York: Viking, 1996.

WEB SITES

Official Web Site of Jack Kerouac
http://www.cmgww.com/historic/Kerouac

Beat Museum Web
www.beatmuseum.org/kerouac

Beat Page Web site
www.rooknet.com/beatpage

Beat Scene Web site
www.beatscene.freeserve.co.uk

Kerouac Speaks Web site:

www.hsc.usc.edu/~gallaher/k_speaks/kerouacspeaks.html

Lite Lit Web site

www.litelit.com/neal.html

Literary Kicks Web site

www.charm.net/~brooklyn/People/JackKerouac.html

National Public Radio Web site

www.npr.org/programs/morning/features/patc/ontheroad

INDEX

JENN MCKEE is a free-lance writer in Berkley, Michigan. She has earned an MFA in creative writing from Penn State and an MA in English from the University of Georgia, and her fiction has appeared in *Prairie Schooner, Passages North*, and the anthology *Best New American Voices 2003*, edited by Joyce Carol Oates.

TOBY THOMPSON teaches English at the Pennsylvania State University where he is a specialist in creative nonfiction, particularly literary journalism. He is a regular contributor to *Vanity Fair, Esquire* and other nationally published magazines, and the author of three books of non-fiction: *Positively Main Street—An Unorthodox View of Bob Dylan* (1971), *Saloon* (1976) and *The 60's Report* (1979).